FLAVORS OF BURMA
MYANMAR

THE HIPPOCRENE COOKBOOK LIBRARY

AFRICA AND OCEANIA
The Best of Regional African
    Cooking
Good Food from Australia
Taste of Eritrea
Traditional South African
    Cookery

ASIA AND
MIDDLE EAST
Afghan Food and Cookery
The Art of Persian Cooking
The Art of Turkish Cooking
The Art of Uzbek Cooking
The Best of Korean Cuisine
The Best of Regional
    Thai Cuisine
The Best of Taiwanese Cuisine
The Cuisine of the
    Caucasus Mountains
Egyptian Cooking
Flavors of Burma
Healthy South
    Indian Cooking
Imperial Mongolian Cooking
The Indian Spice Kitchen
Japanese Home Cooking
Sephardic Israeli Cuisine
A Taste of Syria
A Taste of Turkish Cuisine

MEDITERRANEAN
The Best of Greek Cuisine,
    Expanded Edition
A Spanish Family Cookbook
Taste of Malta
Tastes of North Africa
Tastes of the Pyrenees,
    Classic and Modern

WESTERN EUROPE
The Art of Dutch Cooking,
    Expanded Edition
The Art of Irish Cooking
A Belgian Cookbook
Cooking in the French
    Fashion *(bilingual)*
Cuisines of Portuguese
    Encounters
Feasting Galore Irish-Style
The Scottish-Irish Pub and
    Hearth Cookbook
The Swiss Cookbook
Traditional Food from
    Scotland
Traditional Food from Wales
A Treasury of Italian Cuisine
    (bilingual)

SCANDINAVIA
The Best of Scandinavian
    Cooking
The Best of Finnish Cooking
The Best of Smorgasbord
    Cooking
Icelandic Food & Cookery
Tastes & Tales of Norway

CENTRAL EUROPE
All Along the Rhine
All Along the Danube
The Art of Hungarian
    Cooking
Bavarian Cooking
The Best of Austrian Cuisine
The Best of Czech Cooking
The Best of Polish Cooking
The Best of Slovak Cooking
Hungarian Cookbook
Old Warsaw Cookbook
Old Polish Traditions
Poland's Gourmet Cuisine
The Polish Country Kitchen
    Cookbook
Polish Heritage Cookery
Treasury of Polish Cuisine
    (bilingual)

EASTERN EUROPE
The Art of Lithuanian
    Cooking
The Best of Albanian Cooking
The Best of Croatian Cooking
The Best of Russian Cooking
The Best of Ukrainian Cuisine
Taste of Romania
Taste of Latvia
Traditional Bulgarian Cooking

AMERICAS
Argentina Cooks!
The Art of Brazilian Cookery
The Art of South American
    Cookery
Cooking With Cajun Women
Cooking the Caribbean Way
French Caribbean Cuisine
Mayan Cooking
Old Havana Cookbook
    (bilingual)
A Taste of Haiti
A Taste of Quebec

REFERENCE
International Dictionary of
    Gastronomy

FLAVORS OF BURMA
MYANMAR

Cuisine and Culture
from the Land of Golden Pagodas

SUSAN CHAN

HIPPOCRENE BOOKS
NEW YORK

Photography by Dennis Wong and Mai de Mesa

Book and jacket design by Acme Klong Design, Inc.

For more information, address:
HIPPOCRENE BOOKS, INC.
171 Madison Avenue
New York, NY 10016

ISBN 0-7818-0947-9
Cataloging-in-Publication Data available from the Library of Congress.
Printed in the United States of America.

TABLE OF CONTENTS

ACKNOWLEDGEMENTS

This is a book of traditional Burmese recipes. All have been created, or recreated, in my own kitchen. My visits to Burma have helped reinforce my knowledge.

Naturally, I thank my parents for cooking tirelessly for us for many years and, in the process, teaching me the Burmese style of cooking. I also thank all of those who have helped, in any way, in the production of this book. Particular thanks go to cooks, both amateur and professional, who have shared tips, tastes, and techniques.

I would like to thank my husband, Dennis Wong, for encouraging me to write this book. Even before we were married, we would spend weekends together going shopping for food and creating wonderful meals together. It's a great way to develop a better relationship!!

I would also like to acknowledge, as a source of information, the Welcome to Myanmar handbook on tourism and business issued in April 1995 by the Minister for Information of the Union of Myanmar, His Excellency Brigadier-General Myo Thant.

Other significant sources of information about Burma, which I drew from, were Burmese Culture—General and Particular by U Khin Zaw (1981) and Glimpse of Glorious Pagan by the Department of History at the University of Rangoon (1986).

My thanks also go to my long-term and close friends Mai de Mesa and Patrick Corliss for their invaluable support. Both have always been there to help me. As a native English speaker, Patrick has been particularly valuable as an editor and advisor. Of course, any remaining faults are mine.

I also acknowledge the aid of Hippocrene Books, New York, and its helpful staff, particularly Anne McBride, without whom this book would not have been published.

Finally, I thank my Lord Buddha for making my wish come true in publishing this book. I pray that he will allow me to help Burma, with trade and tourism, and its children with good health and education. I trust that my readers will join with me in a love of this beautiful country.

May all beings in this universe be free from pain and suffering
May they all be free from harm and danger
May they all be well and happy

Susan Chan,
Sydney, Australia, 2002.

INTRODUCTION

Burma is an unusual country in that it tends to be shrouded from the outside world. However, in the past decade or so, it has opened its door to most of its neighbors. In recent years many foreign enterprises have formed joint business ventures with the Burmese government. Singapore, for example, is one country that has built solid relationships through investment in Burmese businesses.

Burma has been blessed with many natural resources. It has an abundance of oil wells, the world's finest teak wood, plentiful rubber plantations, excellent fertile soils for rice fields, mines rich in the world's best jades and rubies, and a profusion of seafood along the coastal areas. In fact, Burma exports all of these products and yet remains a relatively unknown and isolated country.

Burma is becoming a popular tourist destination. According to tourism statistics provided by the Burmese Embassy in Australia (see table on page 3), the past few years have seen a growing number of people visiting Burma. This should not be surprising as Burma has a very interesting history, colorful scenery, and many attractions to explore. One thing lacking, however, is a modern book on Burmese cuisine and culture. My aim is to provide an insight into these two areas.

In this cookbook, I include an overview of the Burmese culture based on experiences from my childhood and my visits to Burma in 1995, 1998, and 2000. I want to share my experience of the food, the culture, the most interesting places I visited, and as well as memories from my early childhood.

In developing this cookbook I was well aware that many people are interested in tasty and nourishing cuisine from exotic locations. To them, the cuisine is most important. However, exotic flavors cannot be isolated from the local culture. The cookbook's two main focuses are:

CUISINE
The cookbook provides a selection of recipes for a variety of well-known Burmese dishes. It is particularly recommended for those intending to travel to Burma so that one can experience the exotic tastes before the trip.

Preparing these delights is both exciting and rewarding. I believe that anyone who follows this book for more than a few recipes will get a good insight into Burma.

CULTURE

A secondary goal is to provide a general background and overview of Burma and its culture. Even if you don't cook, just reading the book will give you an insight into Burmese life. The book includes both recent and historical information as well as details of interesting locations to visit. I hope you get the opportunity to explore some of these places.

I hope that this combination of cuisine and culture provides you with an appreciation of Burma and its culture as well as affording you some pleasant culinary experiences.

FURTHER INFORMATION

Should you have any questions or comments, please visit my website, www.myanmar.com.au, where you can find exciting pictures of Burma and other information.

BURMESE TOURISM FIGURES FOR 1998 AND 1999

(PROVIDED BY THE BURMESE EMBASSY IN AUSTRALIA)

NATIONALITY	1997-1998	Percentage	1998-1999	Percentage
North America	10,991	5.8	13,041	6.5
Canada	1,688	0.9	2,032	1.0
United States	9,303	4.9	11,009	5.5
Latin America	574	0.3	647	0.3
Western Europe	49,400	26.2	52,036	26.0
Austria	1,125	0.6	1,263	0.6
Belgium	2,231	1.2	2,234	1.1
France	17,087	9.1	14,064	7.0
Germany	7,146	3.8	9,396	4.7
Italy	5,631	3.0	6,847	3.4
Switzerland	2,000	1.0	2,517	1.3
U.K.	7,981	4.2	9,577	4.8
Spain	2,022	1.1	1,903	1.0
Other	4,177	2.2	4,235	2.1
Eastern Europe	506	0.3	754	0.4
Russia	143	0.1	213	0.1
Other	363	0.2	541	0.3
Africa	321	0.2	354	0.2
Middle East	1,972	1.0	1,869	0.9
Asia	120,864	64.1	126,441	63.1
Hong Kong	1,340	0.7	1,611	0.8
Japan	34,553	18.3	28,191	14.1
Malaysia	6,987	3.7	6,866	3.4
Singapore	9,606	5.1	10,814	5.4
Thailand	16,297	8.6	20,026	10.0
China	6,047	3.2	9,595	4.8
Taiwan	32,791	17.4	33,154	16.5
Korea	4,847	2.6	5,027	2.5
Bangladesh	389	0.2	752	0.4
India	3,302	1.8	4,474	2.2
Other	4,705	2.5	5,931	3.0
Oceania	4,064	2.1	5,210	2.6
Australia	3,433	1.8	4,499	2.2
New Zealand	642	0.3	711	0.4
TOTALS	188,692	100.0	200,352	100.0

PREFACE

I would briefly like to share with you a little of my background and the reasons that inspired me to write this book.

I was born of Chinese origin in Burma (now called Myanmar). Despite my birth, I was not considered Burmese, as Burmese law does not automatically recognize a person born in Burma as a Burmese citizen. In effect, my family and I were foreigners in our birthplace. Legally we held Chinese passports and did not have the same standing, equalities, or privileges as native Burmese.

My family, composed of my parents, two younger sisters, one brother, and myself, emigrated to Australia in 1976 when I was just a teenager. My father was a carpenter, and at that time, Australia readily accepted people from Burma who had trade skills. Because Australia was almost unknown to most Burmese, his intention was to move before us to assess the situation. The rest of us would then follow upon his recommendation.

However, the Australian embassy in Burma would only allow families to immigrate as one, so we came to Australia together. Only my father understood English at that time and, as is typical with non-English speaking immigrants, we all suffered our share of language problems. We also had to adapt to the new culture we found in Australia. My parents had to work very hard to raise and educate four children. Burmese children are expected to help with cooking and housework, so I was taught to cook simple egg or vegetable rice dishes when I was young.

In Australia, to help my mother after she started work I watched how she prepared her simple but very tasty meals and I began to learn other dishes. I would carefully observe every detail of skinning, chopping, cutting, marinating and cooking. There was a wide variety of meals and a lot to learn. I often kept notes of the ingredients and steps involved so I could reproduce the delicious taste.

My father is also a good cook. With both parents being good cooks, it is not surprising that we love, enjoy and appreciate food. Our parents also spoiled us: Whenever we were craving a particular dish, they usually would cook it that same day.

With a hot and humid climate, and neighbors like India and Thailand, one might expect Burmese dishes to be hot and spicy. This is partially true. However, Burmese dishes have a distinct taste but typically use less spicy ingredients. They are usually quite simple to prepare and cook, and less daunting than other cuisines.

I am sure many of us have experienced the situation where we wanted to try out a new dish that looked fabulously mouthwatering in a book, but were discouraged because it needed unusual ingredients or spices. You may be surprised to find that Burmese dishes are so simple to prepare. Most of the ingredients are already in your kitchen!

I invite you all to have an insight into Burma by trying some of the dishes in this book. Share your new knowledge with your families and friends; introduce them to the recipes. Undoubtedly, you will impress them with your new discoveries about Burma and its mysterious way of life.

BURMA (MYANMAR) IN BRIEF

HISTORICAL BACKGROUND

According to history, Burmese tribes migrated down the river valleys from Tibet and China sometime before A.D. 800 These tribes formed many small kingdoms. In the early eleventh century, one king known as Anawrahta or Anarutha the Great (1044-1077) unified the country and founded the first Burmese empire. So began the Bagan empire that lasted until the thirteenth century.

Even though Buddhism was already well established by the eleventh century, the reign of Anawrahta provided a significant impetus to the development of Buddhism in Burma. This is because King Anawrahta was a man of strong religious zeal as well as being a king of great power. One legend, related by the Department of History at the University of Rangoon in their book *Glimpses of Glorious Pagan*, can be paraphrased as follows:

> *The chronicles relate that a monk from Thaton, Shin Arahan, came to King Anawrahta in Pagan and preached the Law. The monk also taught the king that there could be no study without the scriptures, the Tipitaka, and there were 30 sets at Thaton under the rule of its King Manuha.*
>
> *The king was seized with an ecstasy of faith and sent an envoy with presents to Manuha, asking for the Tipitaka. When Manuha declined, Anawrahta sent a mighty army, conquered Thaton, and seized the Tipitaka. These were brought back, with Manuha and his court, on 32 white elephants.*

This Bagan Empire encompassed most of the present-day Myanmar and included the entire Menam Valley in Thailand. In 1287, Kublai Khan's Mongol armies captured Bagan and gained control of this empire. This lasted until 1303 when Burma again broke up into small kingdoms.

King Tabinshweti (d.1551) and his able successor King Bayinnaung united the country and founded the second Burmese empire in mid-sixteenth century. The third and last Burmese dynasty was founded by King Alaungpaya (1711-1760) in 1752 after conquering almost all of present-day Burma.

Between 1824 and 1826, to protect the security of India, British troops drove the Burmese out of eastern India and took over parts of Burma. In 1852, in a second Anglo-Burmese war, the British seized the rest of lower Burma. Finally, in the third and last war, the British captured Mandalay in 1885. Within a year Burma became a province of India and one of the British colonies.

During the Second World War, the Japanese occupied Burma for three years from 1942 until the return of the Allied Forces in 1945. Although the last country occupied by the British in Southeast Asia, Burma was the first country to gain her independence. Burma became independent on January 4, 1948, after 62 years of colonial administration. The military government changed the official name of the country from Burma to the Union of Myanmar on June 19, 1989. Although this name is changed and recognized by the United Nations, many people still refer to it as Burma, which I myself prefer.

MAP OF BURMA

The outline of Burma reminds me of the outline of a happy smiling person. He is facing west; he has a high forehead, curve of the nose, and a smiling lip; followed by a double chin, fat body up to the tummy finishing off with stumpy legs. In high school geography, I drew so many maps of Burma by hand that I could quickly reproduce the shape almost exactly. Others say that Burma looks like a kite with a tail. I can see what they mean but I prefer my way of looking at Burma.

MAP
OF
MYANMAR

GEOGRAPHY AND CLIMATE

Burma is divided into upper and lower regions. Upper Burma, containing mountains, valleys and forests, comprises most of the country. Lower Burma, which includes the entire 1,650-mile coastline, is significant for its river systems and natural resources. To get some perspective, Burma's total area is 261,218 square miles, making it the largest country in the Southeast Asian peninsula. It is about twice the size of Vietnam.

Burma is located on the north shore of the Bay of Bengal. In clockwise order, Burma shares borders with Bangladesh and India (to the east), China (north and north-east), Laos (west), and Thailand (south-west).

The average temperatures range from 19 to 38 degrees Celsius or from 38 to 76 degrees Fahrenheit. Generally, Burma is cool in the mountains and hot and wet in areas near the coast. In the mountains the temperature can fall below freezing during the winter.

Burma basically has three seasons: hot season from March to May; rainy season (due to the monsoon effect) from June to October; and cool season from November to February. The cool season is generally considered the best time to visit Burma.

Burma experiences monsoon rains in different parts of the country at different times. Monsoon winds starting in May bring heavy rains to the western sides of the mountains of upper Burma, as well as to the lower parts of the country.

BURMESE CULTURE

LANGUAGE AND PEOPLE

Burma is a union of numerous nationalities speaking over a hundred different languages or dialects. The country is divided into seven states; each of which represents a different race or ethnic group. The major races are Kachin, Kayah, Kayin, Chin, Bamar, Mon, Rakhine, and Shan. While each of these has its own customs, beliefs, language, and dress, the Mons have had the greatest influence on present-day Burmese culture, literature, and sculpture.

In fact, the Burmese language is based on the one spoken by the Mon people, whose civilization was already established before the time of King Anawrahta. Through them, the Burmese adapted the writing, which later became the country's first official language. The alphabet has 33 syllables; each syllable is combined with diacritical marks to create different meanings.

English is widely spoken in the major cities of Rangoon (Yangon), Mandalay, and Bagan. Cantonese and Mandarin are also widely spoken because of the large Chinese population of Burma.

According to the latest available figures, the population of Burma is now around 47 million.

RELIGION

Novices meditating

During the eleventh century, under the reign of King Anawrahta, Buddhism came from Thaton to Bagan. Over the next 200 years, during the Bagan Empire, there was a strong influence of Buddhism in Burmese life. This can be seen in the architecture, painting, and sculpture depicted in the Buddhist temples throughout Bagan.

Buddhism has had a major influence on the tradition and attitude of the Burmese people. In fact after centuries of Buddhism, it is quite impossible to distinguish between cultural and religious influences. These include worshipping Buddha, maintaining close family ties, and paying respect to their elders. While the majority of people in the country is Buddhist, people of the Kayin race are mainly Christian. Other major religions, such as Islam and Hinduism, are also represented in Burma.

NAMING CONVENTIONS

One interesting aspect about Burmese names is that the Burmese people simply do not have any family names. To fully identify a person, both parents' names must be mentioned. Otherwise, there is no unique way to identify that person. In general conversation, a person is customarily identified through either or both parents as "who-and-who's son" or "who-and-who's daughter."

Let's take one name for example, Aung Sung Suu Kyi, the Nobel Prize winner. Her own personal name is Suu Kyi (pronounced "Sujee") and she is generally known as Aung Sung Suu Kyi after her father, the late General Aung Sung.

The traditional naming convention is such that it is not polite to call someone by his or her name without any title or honorific. In childhood or youth, a boy is called "Maung" followed by his name and a girl is "Ma" followed by her name. When older, married, or in a position of importance, men are called "U" and women "Daw" before their names.

As a girl, Suu Kyi would have been called "Ma Suu Kyi." After her marriage, the word "Ma" is replaced by "Daw." She is then called "Daw Suu Kyi." With her father's name, I think rightfully with respect, she should be called "Daw Aung Sun Suu Kyi."

In a similar case, a man with a personal name of "Win Kyi" (pronounced "Winjee") would be called "Maung Win Kyi" before marriage and "U Win Kyi" afterward.

This Burmese custom shows respect to an older or more distinguished person. A single man or woman can be entitled "U" or "Daw" depending on their occupational status. For example, school teachers are highly respected and thus a young female teacher is also referenced as "Daw" although she is single. So it is sometimes difficult to know whether a person is married or not.

SCHOOLS

The education system in Burma encourages people to compete. It is based on traditional concepts of learning and respect for your teacher. Like elsewhere in the world, the system is divided into schools and universities. School fees are cheap enough but universities can be much more expensive.

When I was a child in Burma, schools had two sessions per day, one from 7 a.m. to noon and another from noon to 5 p.m. A normal school session started with a bell that rang for classes to commence and to close the school gate. Anyone late for school had to sweep the floor and clean up the classroom after class, as a means of punishment. The bell also alerted students to make their daily prayers.

Even today, when the teacher enters the classroom, it is customary to stand up and greet the teacher by saying "mingalabar sayar" (for a male teacher) or "mingalabar sayarma" (for a female teacher). The word *mingalabar* mean "good blessing" and is a respectful greeting for your teacher.

Students advance to the next grade only if they pass the exam set at the end of each year. Otherwise, they must repeat the same grade the following year.

As in many Asian countries, teachers are highly respected by both parents and students. Corporal punishment with a cane or ruler is very much accepted by all. This is a common method used to improve students' performance and behavior.

In the mid-seventies, a major drive to increase literacy among the Burmese people at large was introduced by the government. As part of this process, many university students volunteered to live in rural areas, during their summer vacation, and teach basic Burmese language skills. This was particularly successful in encouraging older people to participate in the program.

DRESS AT SCHOOLS AND UNIVERSITIES

One thing worth mentioning is the Burmese school uniform. From primary to high schools, all students and teachers, both male or female, wear the same colors. Like elsewhere in the world, uniforms consist of two parts. The top is a blouse or shirt and this is always white. The bottom may be a *longyi*, worn by either sex, or a skirt worn by females only. The *longyi* is a wraparound piece of material that fully covers the area between the waist and the ankle. The way it is worn differs between the sexes: men tie a knot in the front, women tuck the material to the side. Standard colors are always white and dark green.

Everybody wearing the same color uniform creates a fascinating scene throughout Burma. The school dismissal flood of white and green led one Burmese writer to describe the scene as similar to a "sprinkle of jasmine flowers." Of course, jasmine, with its white flowers and dark green leaves, is one of Burma's favorite flowers. I think this beautiful analogy is worth sharing.

Throughout their school life, students wear these standard uniforms but once they get to the university level, there is a significant change in dress standards especially among females. In this new environment, women dress up as if for a special occasion in fashionable clothes, jewelry, and cosmetics. The focus is on competing for attention as well getting an education.

When I was young, I looked forward to going to the university, where I could dress up and be a member of this smart and elite group of young people. I came to Australia as a teenager and completed my studies there and here. When I went to the university, all students dressed very casually, often in jeans and T-shirts. This is very different from the style in Burma. At that point I really felt sorry for the poor students in Burma who often feel inferior and find it hard to compete in a system that I now see as amusing.

Danaka

BURMESE NATIONAL COSMETIC: *DANAKA*
In Burma, it is common to see female students, teachers, and even young children paint their cheeks and noses with pale yellow or bright yellow paste. This traditional Burmese cosmetic cools the body, reduces facial oil, and adds brightness. This paste is ground from the bark of a tree called *danaka*. The tree trunk is quite slim about the diameter of a teacup. Sections of the trunk, or logs, are sold throughout the country. The tree itself has yellow flowers in the shape of tiny beads. These are so fragile that shaking

even a single stem causes lots of tiny yellow beads to sprinkle.

Making the paste is a traditional and common task. This is done by rubbing a log in a circular motion against a smooth grinding-stone. This stone is flat, round, and about 10 centimeters (4 inches) in diameter. The paste is quite thick so a dash of water is added to thin the paste. When ready, the paste is scooped with either of the first two fingers, and spread across the cheeks, nose, and forehead. After that, the remaining paste is scooped by hand and applied to the arms and legs.

When I was at school in Burma, I performed this task every day before going to school. As you need a clean face and body, this paste is only applied after having a shower. My preference was for a thinner paste lightly applied. I would use a clean toothbrush to smooth the surface. This also gave a neat appearance with tiny brush-strokes on my face and nose.

Today, shops all over Burma sell ready-made powder that just needs to have water added. Of course, this instant method cannot match the traditional technique of grinding the paste yourself.

WEDDING CEREMONY: MINGALARSONG

In a traditional wedding ceremony, the Burmese people wear colorful costumes. The costume for the groom consists of a headband or a turban, a Burmese jacket, a *longyi* (a long piece of material wrapped from the waist down to the ankle), and platform velvet thongs. The costume for the bride consists of a long-sleeved wedding blouse, a *longyi*, a transparent head-dress or shawl, and platform velvet thongs. Materials are hand woven in silk.

Wedding costumes

Burmese women are very fond of flowers and wear flowers on their heads. On this occasion, they style their hair and put on beautiful and exotic flowers such as orchids or roses. Other adornments include ruby or sapphire jewels to complement the wedding costume. Burma is famous the world over for its rubies. Different grades and qualities can be purchased in any major market. At the famous Scott's Market in Rangoon, many jewelry shops sell rubies, sapphires, and jades.

During the ceremony, the marriage celebrant pronounces the couple to be husband and wife and blesses them to have a long and enduring marriage. Traditionally, monks from the local Buddhist monastery are invited to the wedding ceremony. In a good wedding, up to ten monks will chant and bless the newlyweds with scented flower water.

Following the ceremony, food is served. The monks are served first, then the more elderly people, then friends, and finally the family. Usually, the food is served mid-morning as brunch.

The wedding reception is either a banquet held in an expensive restaurant or a more simple affair held at home. Choice of venue often depends on the financial status of the bride and groom or their respective families. As a general rule, the groom's family will bear the expense but both families will provide the couple with generous gifts, sometimes including valuable jewelry, a new house or car, depending on their status.

This follows the Burmese belief in the duties of parents to raise and educate their children. The final step in this process is to find a suitable partner for their child and set them up for a happy future. In Burma today, there are still many arranged marriages but some children do rebel against the system and elope to get married. When this occurs, it usually causes parents to disown their children with a formal notice to that effect being placed in the newspapers.

A wedding ceremony, especially one held at home, will serve Coconut Chicken Noodle Soup (see page 195), pronounced "Ohn-Noh-Khauk-Swei." This traditional wedding dish needs to be prepared the night before by families and friends. As well as being a tradition in weddings, this dish is also very popular as a breakfast meal served to the public in market stalls and restaurants.

NEW YEAR WATER FESTIVAL: THINGYAN

Burma, with its own calendar, has many festivals throughout the year. The Burmese New Year festival is one of the merriest and indeed a most eventful one. This festival coincides with the monsoon rain season, which is around April. This is the hottest time of the year and the weather only becomes a little cooler with the arrival of Monsoon rain. New Year is the time for people to have an opportunity to celebrate and have fun.

The traditional festival is celebrated over three significant days throughout the country. Many people wait excitedly for the arrival of the festival as there is so much fun and plenty of good food. A large bamboo thatched hall is built temporarily in most streets. Here, volunteers make New Year sweets such as small glutinous rice dumplings with palm sugar cubes inside, coated with grated coconut outside. One refreshing drink is Sweet and Sour Tamarind Juice (page 211), served with ice cubes. This is popular to quench the hot summer thirst.

Such confectioneries and drinks are offered to people passing by. Loudspeakers are attached in these large thatched halls. New Year songs can be heard everywhere and joyous people sing and dance to this occasion. Large tanks filled with water are used to splash or pour water over people as they pass. Out of respect, elderly people, babies, and pregnant mothers are exempt. Young and single persons especially delight in splashing water on the opposite sex. Children love this occasion because they have a chance to play with water in the hot weather.

Buddhists believe that pouring water cleanses the body and mind of evils of the previous year. In the olden days, the traditional approach was to pour some water over a person's shoulder gently after asking for permission to do so. Today the traditional gentle approach has almost disappeared and teenagers are a lot more daring. Water hoses are occasionally used and beautiful girls are the targets for men or boys, who water them until they are totally soaked. No harm is meant and young people are very excited about riding in a jeep or a car and getting wet.

In a quieter way, elderly and religious devotees perform meritorious deeds to usher in an auspicious New Year. They offer food and robes to the monks and some people stay in temples for a few days or weeks to meditate. People pay their respects by offering food and presents. The highest order of respect is paid to the Lord Buddha. Others, in descending order of respect, are monks, parents, and school teachers. Children, in particular, are taught to pay their respects to parents, teachers, and elders.

NEW YEAR FLOWERS: PADAUK

The Burmese New Year is also the time when basket flowers (*padauk*) are in season. These huge trees are filled with bright yellow flowers. The flowers, which only blossom over the New Year, are very sweet and fragrant. At this time, they are abundant and their bright color lights up the scene everywhere. In fact, during the festive season, the whole country is filled with these flowers. They are used to decorate temples, thatched halls, shops, houses, cars, and jeeps. Everywhere is filled with these vibrant and fragrant flowers. Women and girls even put bunches of bright yellow flowers in their hair.

The basket flower is a popular tree for many other reasons. Its trunk is used for making handicrafts and these are sold almost everywhere in Burma. In addition, *padauk* parquetry is a popular floor covering that is exported to many countries around the world.

Youk-thay

BURMESE MARIONETTE SHOW: YOUK-THAY

In Burma, the marionette show is a traditional form of entertainment consisting of full-length dramas presented to audiences. These shows are a serious art form consisting of marionettes that range in size from a small doll to full adult-sized substitutes for human players. Whatever their size, marionettes are expertly manipulated so they appear to come to life and perform the show by themselves. Years of practice are needed to make the show look as life-like as possible.

A marionette has numerous strings attached. Each string has a specific task to achieve different movements and gestures such as to sing, dance, speak, and even to portray emotions. The marionette can be a prince, princess, monkey, hermit, or any other figure. I remember watching one show where a real person was dancing on the left side of the stage and an adult-sized marionette was dancing on the right side of the stage. During this routine, the marionette followed and appeared to copy the human dancer exactly in both steps and movements. The human and the marionette look so much alike that it was difficult to tell them apart. The skill needed to do this was truly remarkable.

In 1998, when I stayed at a hotel in Bagan, a marionette show was the highlight of the night's entertainment. An old man handled the marionette on a small stage. The lights were out and the marionette performed a dance by candlelight. In fact, the marionette held a real lit candle on the palm of each hand. This old man pulled and manipulated the strings with such expertise that the marionette not only kept the candles alight but also managed to avoid burning the supporting strings.

Marionette shows are often recorded on video, which affords many people the opportunity to be entertained. I have seen these myself and hope that you can, too. But I highly recommend trying to see a live Burmese marionette show if you ever get the opportunity.

Saung-kauk

BURMESE HARP: SAUNG-KAUK

The traditional Burmese harp, the *saung hauk*, is shaped like a boat but curvier. This beautiful harp is colored gold and decorated with tiny red, blue, and green mirrors which resemble precious jewels such as rubies, jades, and emeralds. The harp has many strings stretched from the base to the top curvature. Red tassels are attached to the upper ends of the strings and these hang beautifully to enhance the gracefulness of the harp.

Usually, the harp is placed on a specially made stand. At home, the whole set is place on a cabinet where it can been seen from a distance. The harp is treated respectfully and never left lying around on the floor. These instruments are handmade and usually quite expensive.

When being played, the strings are gently plucked with left or right thumb and fingers to produce different musical notes. The harp is held against the chest and rests on the lap. A female player will sit modestly on the floor with both knees folded together and feet tucked away.

In the olden days, people would often be seen leisurely playing the harp on a verandah under the moonlight. This could be to relax and enjoy the music, soothe the emotions, or welcome a lover.

INTERESTING PLACES IN BURMA

Yangon

YANGON (RANGOON)
In 1755, during the last dynasty, King Alaungpaya conquered Dagon. This was the most important locality in lower Burma due to its geographic location and abundant natural resources. The king changed the name of the town from Dagon to Yangon, which means "end of strife," to signify an end to the constant war among people.

I was born in Rangoon and lived in a well-known township called Kamayuat. This is only fifteen to twenty minutes by car from the city center. Rangoon is the capital city in Burma where mostly Burmese, Chinese, and Indian people reside.

I had always wanted to visit the region known as upper Burma. However, my family left Burma in 1976 before I had the chance. It was only in 1995 that I went back to Burma with a friend to carry out my childhood wish.

My first visit was an interesting experience. With the help of my parents' friends, my friend and I went to many of the places that I describe below. The second trip (in 1998) included Kyattiyo, Pegu, Bagan, and Yangon.

Let me start with my trip from Yangon. I'll describe a tour around Yangon starting from the International Rangoon airport, where flights are mostly from Thailand, Singapore, and Hong Kong. This airport was refurbished and upgraded for the 1996 "Visit Burma" year, in an attempt to boost tourism.

From the airport, we began our journey to the city of Rangoon. The first thing we noticed were the very wide roads due to the earlier British settlement and influence. They are also quite clean. A twenty-minute minivan journey led to Main University Road where the Yangon University is situated beside the University Lake. Another fifteen minutes took us to the main U-Visaya Road, where a big roundabout or circular intersection (a British influence) contains a large pillar surmounted by the statue of a respected monk (also named U-Visaya).

Shwedagon Pagoda

Shwedagon Pagoda

Far away from here, one can see the Shwedagon pagoda ("Golden pagoda in the Dagon city") towering above the city of Yangon. This great golden pagoda, which is a major attraction in Yangon, rises about 100 meters (327 feet) above its base and is believed to have been built about 2,500 years ago.

There are four divisions of the pagoda: the east, west, north and southern divisions. The stairways leading up from the base are made from tiles and are lined with small shops selling items such as lacquer handicrafts, books, and flowers. Once on the plinth, it is customary to tour around the central part of the pagoda in a clockwise direction. This accords with the Burmese Buddhist belief.

Numerous statues of the Lord Buddha, ogres, and ogresses, guard the temples, while angel deva, fairy, goddess, and sakka images can be seen everywhere in the large temple compound. Teak pillars, expertly carved by skillful sculptors, portray ancient art and architecture. The Buddhist exhibition hall displays many Buddha images, icons, arts, handicrafts, and a replica of the Shwedagon pagoda. It is quite beyond words to describe this majestic pagoda and I can only recommend a visit if you have the opportunity. In fact it is worth visiting Burma just to experience this awe-inspiring sight.

The pagoda is always packed with people who come to worship the Lord Buddha. Many people, especially the elderly, come and pray in the morning as early as five o'clock. It is believed that early praying and meditation bring the pilgrim more good deeds but I am sure that many adopt this practice because the weather is cooler and the pagoda less crowded at that early hour.

Most elderly people, monks, nuns, and novices meditate using prayer beads. Many candles are lit in the early morning and these create an extremely peaceful atmosphere.

Evening is also a good time to visit the pagoda, because the weather is cooler and invites one to relax and enjoy one's self after a hard day's work.

In a clockwise direction there are seven sets of pagodas, one for each day of the week. This is significant to Burmese as they associate their birthday with a particular day of the week. Each day is also associated with an animal and people relate their birthday to the relevant animal sign. Monday, for example, is associated with the tiger and Tuesday, the lion. The other days are Wednesday (elephant), Thursday (rat), Friday (pig), Saturday (dragon) and Sunday (phoenix). People pray and pay respects in all seven pagodas but perform extra rituals in the pagoda corresponding with their birthday. They bathe the Buddha by pouring water over him, which symbolizes cleansing one's bad deeds and at the same time, bringing peace and purity to the mind. People also offer flowers and light candles, and donate money. Vases are always filled with offered fragrant flowers such as flock, roses, star flowers, jasmine, gladiola, dahlia, wormwood plant flowers, and yellow ginger lily flower. The most popular flower is the eugenia. This looks more like a leaf than a flower and is believed to bring soldiers safely back from the battlefield.

From the Shwedagon pagoda we visited some of the Burmese restaurants selling authentic and tasty dishes at the base of the pagoda. As all meals have been precooked, it is almost like a fast-food service.

First served, as side dishes, are the assorted raw and boiled vegetables. These are dipped into Burma's most famous fermented fish sauce, which has a strong fragrance and a salty taste. One will either like it or hate it.

Be warned that all the dishes come in small portions. We had to order a few servings of our favorite dishes. This does not matter, as everything is very cheap. Ten U.S. dollars easily fed six of us, including the driver, with delicious and tasty food. For our meal, we had Mock Curry Prawns (or rather shrimp), Fried Roselle Leaves, Mango Salad, Chicken and Vermicelli Soup, and Steamed Hilsha Fish. So as to digest our heavy lunch, we decided to walk around the town's main market.

Scott Market

This market, built in 1926, was initially named Scott Market after the then municipal commissioner, Mr. C. Scott. Officially, the name was later changed to Bogyoke Aung San Market in honor of General Aung San, the national leader who was assassinated in 1947. General Aung San is also well known as the father of Nobel prizewinner, Aung San Sui Kyi. The name Scott Market seems to live on regardless.

In this market, there are many shops selling luxury items, handicrafts, foodstuffs, clothing, jewelry, and fashion and consumer goods. The jewelry shops specialize in Burma's most precious gems, such as ruby, sapphire, and emerald. Of course, the price of these stones varies with the quality. Many handicrafts are made from different trees such as basket flower tree (*padauk*), teak, sandalwood, or bamboo. The quality of these wares is generally good and the prices are most reasonable.

There are also several modern department stores in and around the city areas and many products are from Japan, Thailand, and China. There are many shops along the main roads of the city and it takes almost a day to shop them all.

City Center

In the city center, another popular pagoda is the Swela pagoda. Other attractions are the museum and Chinatown. Most city buildings show the influence of British architecture and this is also apparent from the roads, which are very wide. In the evening when the heat subsided, we strolled along Chinatown where many shops and roadside stalls start business in the late afternoon. We had a great time shopping and bargaining in the mini-markets, gold shops, and many others. For dinner, we selected one of the Chinese restaurants in Chinatown. In this area, there is a most respected Chinese temple where many Chinese go to worship.

When I was quite young, perhaps about seven or eight years old, my grandmother would take me to pray in this temple. I remember I was always scared of the very loud noise from a big drum that beat every few minutes. When I went back to the temple in 1995, I found the drumbeat just as loud and ominous as before. But at least I was no longer scared of the sound!

More Pagodas

Malamu Pagoda

On our visit, we also went to the Malamu pagoda, which is about thirty minutes by car from the city. There we saw very many giant Buddha statues portraying Buddha preaching. There are many other interesting places to visit in Yangon and not enough space here for me to describe everything. I would strongly advise that you go and see it for yourself.

A journey of under an hour from the city takes you to a popular temple called Yele Paya. This is a pagoda built in the middle of the water. On the way there, we crossed over a bridge that was built by the Chinese people. To reach to the pagoda situated in the middle of the muddy water, we took a ten-minute ride in a small boat. This boat was rowed manually by the owner using a single oar. The river is teeming with fish that live on popcorn fed to them by visitors.

Many visitors offer gold leaves to adorn the Buddha. Like them, my friends and I bought some gold leaves. We then put them into a little cart and pulled the pulley until it reached the top of the pagoda. At the top of the pagoda, the arrival of gold is announced by the noise of the bells on the cart as it travels.

In Burma, most temple donations are used for maintenance. Funds are often used to purchase tiles for the temple footpaths. Rich and generous people usually donate large sums of money or build new temples to show their strong belief, respect, and faith in Buddhism.

Kamayut Township

During our second visit to Burma, we stayed in Kamayuat for a few days at our friends' apartment near the highway. From their balcony we had a good view of the passing traffic. Transportation is still quite poor and most of the vehicles are older-style trucks and buses. Nonetheless during peak hours they are all fully loaded. Passengers are allowed to get in as long as there is something that they can grip and hold on to. In the early morning, we could also see Buddhist monks following one another to get their day's offerings. One reason why housewives usually cook at early dawn is so that food is ready to be offered to the monks. Burmese monks will only eat before noon; after that time, no food can be eaten until the next day after dawn.

In Kamayuat, the main market was just two minutes away from where we stayed. In this market there is a Burmese temple and an Indian temple. I found that the market area had not changed much after 20 years and that those temples were still there.

Several high-rise buildings replaced the old houses that were demolished to make way for the highway in preparation for "Visit Burma Year" in 1996. My former high school was still there but all the surrounding houses, including our old house, had been demolished and replaced by six-story units.

PEGU (BAGO)

Lacquered food carrier

South of Rangoon, another popular destination in Burma is the town of Pegu, located in the "Mon" state. Mon people first settled in this town and it is about an hour by car from Rangoon. Along this journey, we could see new roads being constructed. Rice fields could be seen in the distance. The main attraction in Pegu is a giant reclining Buddha, known as the Shwethalyaung Buddha.

Most people come here to pray and have a picnic. Usually, people cook at home and then bring their lunch in a tiered food container. This useful utensil is made from stainless steel, aluminum, enamel or lacquer. Visitors find a nice, cool spot at the foot of the Buddha and lunch there.

When I was in primary and high school, students would often visit the reclining Buddha on school excursions. Even today, parties of school children are frequent visitors there. Bago is also particularly popular for artists and photographers.

Shwethalyaung Buddha

This giant reclining Buddha is awesome. Its impressive dimensions are as follows:

Subject	Meters	Feet	Subject	Meters	Feet
Length	54.88	180	Shoulder to Waist	14.48	47.5
Height	16	52.5	Waist to Knee	14.48	47.5
Face	6.86	22.5	Knee to Foot	14.48	47.5
Ear	4.57	15	Elbow to Tip of Finger	13.71	45
Eye	1.14	3.75	Little Finger	3.05	10
Eye Brow	2.29	7.5	Sole of Foot	7.77	225.5
Eye Lid	2.29	7.5	Great Toe	1.83	6
Nose	2.29	7.5	Palm of Hand	6.71	22
Lip	2.29	7.5			
Neck	2.29	7.5			

Note: 1 Meter = 3.28 feet

KYAIKTIYO PAGODA

Another famous attraction is the giant leaning rock statue situated on top of a mountain about 3600 feet above sea level, in a town called Kyaikto. This is about five hours by car from Yangon, passing through Pegu (Bago). Legend has it that this rock resembles the head of a great hermit who lived and meditated on this mountain many years ago.

When the great Lord Buddha passed thorough this place on his preaching journey, he presented a few strands of his hair to this hermit. The hermit, who had attained magical power, tried to find some rocks to resemble his head. The hermit finally retrieved a rock that closely resembled his head out of the deep ocean. He then placed this giant rock on top of the mountain, at the edge, so that it barely leaned and touched the mountainside.

Mounted on this rock is an ornamental shrine, or *stupa*, where the Buddha's hair is enshrined and worshipped. It is also believed that a giant dragon guards the mountain and there are many animals living in this mountain as well.

When I was twelve, I went to Kyaiktiyo. At that time, I had to climb up from the base of the mountain to the top on foot. It took me about five hours to climb with the help of a walking stick that I bought at the bottom.

Only in recent years have roads been constructed for vehicles to climb up as close as possible to the top of the mountain. However, the rough road did not permit our car to climb up easily. Twice we had to get out of the car so that it would be light enough to move.

When it became too steep for the car, we continued the journey on foot for about an hour. There were many carriers who competed to carry luggage in woven cane baskets or carry passengers on a stretcher, for a very small price.

On this trip, we began our climb at about 7:30 p.m. when it was quite dark. However, it was a very peaceful place. When we looked up at the sky, it seemed that we were very close to the hundreds of bright stars. We reached our destination in darkness at about 8:30 p.m. and stayed in the only motel with western facilities.

After we washed and dined, we walked up to the leaning rock statue to pray. As we approached the temple near the leaning rock we could see bright lights and many people praying or simply sleeping with only blankets. There was also a traditional performance with Burmese costumes and music.

When we got close to the leaning rock statue, we were a little disappointed to find that the statue had been completely covered with mats for maintenance. When we asked, we were told that this was done every three years to prevent the wind from blowing away the gold leaves that were offered by people and to allow some time for the leaves to stick to the statue.

With the coverings, we could only see the tall *stupa* sticking out of the mats. Still it was awesome to see a giant rock with its base just touching and leaning onto the mountain edge. There was a small bridge over which only men were allowed to walk to get closer to this respected statue (according to Burmese belief, women are not allowed to cross). It is quite cold on top of the mountain and after spending some time watching the traditional dance show, we headed back to the room.

The next morning, we got up at about 5:30 a.m. to see the sun rise. While we were waiting, we sat on very low wooden stools in a tea shop. Then, at about six o'clock, we witnessed a beautiful and serene view of the sun rising above the mountain. It was then time to go back to the pagoda for a final visit.

We also went to a place called Crow's Mouth by walking up and down winding steep pathways. This is a giant rock resembled the shape of a big crow's beak. When we arrived we saw people throwing coins in to make wishes. Before the sun got too hot, we returned to our room, then descended the mountain and headed back to Rangoon via Bago (Pegu).

Bagan

BAGAN

A visit to Burma is not complete without a visit to Bagan, the land of a Thousand Buddhist Statues and Temples. This important archaeological area is situated in central

Burma on the eastern bank of the Irrrawaddy (Ayerwaddy) River. Bagan covers 16 square miles and attracts visitors from all over the world. It is an hour by plane from Yangon.

Buddhism has had great influence in Burma, especially during ancient times when royal kings or wealthy people built big and awe-

Bagan pagoda

some temples to show their dedication, respect, and faith in the religion, and promote Bagan as a royal city. It is a Buddhist belief that such wholesome deeds bring good karma to the kingdom.

Within the city, a person can stand anywhere and point a finger in any direction to find a temple. However, many trees and acres of forests have been cleared to build these temples. Over time, what used to be a green city and plain almost resembles a desert, hot, dry, and practically treeless. However, during my second visit I noticed that the government and the people have started to plant some trees around the city and around the temples.

The headwaiter in the Kumudara Hotel where we stayed, told us jokingly that "in the olden days powerful and rich people competed to show their wealth by building bigger and larger temples. Nowadays, they compete with larger and bigger hotels and motels to show their wealth."

In 1975 however, an earthquake ruined thousands of these age-old temples and now it is estimated only about two thousand temples remain. Bagan is still one of the most popular tourist destinations in Burma. To this day, Bagan is a sight to behold and is a most inspired archaeological area. Some temples are more than 200 years old; some of the older ones even have the Buddha image defaced. Occasionally, there are images of proud men on horseback said to have been drawn by the once invading Mongol armies.

As it could take many days to tour this ancient city to visit all the temples, most visitors will not have enough time. At each temple, local people sell various colorful handicrafts such as trays, bowls, and small tables that are produced in Bagan.

The Irrawaddy (Ayerwaddy) River, Burma's longest and most important river, flows alongside some of these temples. One evening, we sat on a bench in the Bupaya pagoda to watch the beautiful sunset along the Irrawaddy River. In Burmese, 'bu' means "gourd," and 'paya' means "pagoda." Thus 'bupaya' is shaped like a gourd. The Bupaya pagoda is a distinct white pagoda situated high near the river and is a popular destination.

Another night, we climbed to the top of the Shewsandaw Temple with many other tourists, to watch a most spectacular sunset over Bagan, the Irrawaddy river, and the surrounding mountains and plains. Shewsandaw means "gold hair strand" or translated as "golden holy hair relic," because the Lord Buddha's holy hair relic is enshrined in a *stupa* at the top the pagoda.

There were five square terraces, shaped like a pyramid and ascended by very steep stairways. However, there was no handrail to hold. As I climbed up each step, my legs trembled and I could reach only the first terrace, while others continued to the second and even to the last terrace. I walked along the four corners of the temple and enjoyed the peaceful views of Bagan. At around 6 p.m., all the tourists gathered, ready to watch the magnificent sunset and take pictures.

Mount Popa

MOUNT POPA

From Bagan, an hour by car took us to Mount Popa. From the base of the mountain, one need to climb 777 steps to reach the mountaintop. At the base of the mountain, girls rushed up to sell their flowers to the tourists. There was no end to the buying as each girl kept begging for us to buy from her as well.

As we climbed, we could see many monkeys in the nearby trees. When we came back to the base of the mountain, there was a Nat ceremony nearby and we decided to pay it a visit. Both men and women in colorful costume danced to pay respects to Nat. Nat is a spirit worshiped by people who believe that by paying respect and offering ceremonies to the Nat, they will in turn be protected.

MANDALAY

Mandalay, established in 1857, is the second largest city of Myanmar. It was the capital city before Yangoon. The attractions in this city are the great Maha Muni Pagada, the Royal Palace, and the famous Mandalay hilltop, where a panoramic view of the city can be seen. The Mandalay hill rises 236 meters (775 feet) above the city and is located in the northeast of the palace. Mandalay produces goods and famous food such as Mandalay Chicken Noodle (page 207), known as Mandalay Mouti, a delicious dish consisting of noodles and chicken pieces.

SHAN STATE (DHAUNGI, INLE, KALAW, PYIN-OO-LWIN)

During my 1995 visit, we went to Bagan by van. We flew to Heho airport (about 1½ hours from Yangon) and then were picked up by a friend's car to get to Dhaungi. Dhaungi is situated in upper Burma, north of Rangoon, which is the capital of Shan State. Dhaungi means "big mountain" and beautiful scenic views can be seen from its top. Here, the weather is cool and it becomes very cold during winter.

From Dhaungi, we traveled to Inle Lake by van. Inle Lake is about 22 kilometers long, 10 kilometers wide (13 by 6 miles), and 900 meters (2,700 ft.) above sea level. The water is very calm and it is a very famous and peaceful scenic place surrounded by mountains. The Inle people build bamboo houses and live on the water. Fishing by a net or using a sharp bamboo spear is the most prominent activity in this area and fish is the main food. One unique thing about these people is that they row their boat using one leg, which wraps around the long oar and the other leg is firmly placed on the boat.

One most famous temple in Inle Lake has a set of five little Buddha statues. These statues have lost their original shapes due to excessive gold leaf offerings. They now look like little fat golden gourds and they are known as '"Bu" (gourd) pagodas as well.

We had lunch at a nearby monastery. Usually the monks cook the food or people cook and offer food to the monks. It was still touching to know that the monks and the people are generous and kind enough to offer us free lunch. We were so hungry and the dishes were good. We donated some money to repay the monastery's kindness.

Inle is famous for producing beautiful weaving products such as longyi, which is clothing worn by the people. The Inle shoulder bag or the national bag is very famous and is carried—draped over the shoulder—by students, office and non-office workers, young or old. Colorful and beautiful *longyi* as well as bags with beads can be purchased in this area.

We continued our journey to Kalaw. This is a beautiful and scenic area with pine trees planted along the roads and is a breath of fresh air and very quiet. Early morning mists make this area very peaceful and tranquil. Kalaw has western country appearance due to its western influence.

Kale and Dhaungi are popular cities in Shan State because of cooler weather and many songs have been written to describe these places. They usually describe the beautiful Shan girls with their dimple smiles and rosy cheeks, their friendliness, their different accents and the way they speak. Other love songs tell of the Burmese boys falling in love with the beautiful and kind Shan girls while visiting Kalaw or Dhaungi.

Shan State is also popular for its Shan Noodle and the soft and tasty Shan Tofu dishes.

As we traveled south to Pyin-Oo-Lwin, the weather warmed. This area is famous for nice weather and the attractions are a waterfall, the botanical garden, and hundreds of Buddha statues built inside a narrow and long cave called Bait-Chin-Myoung.

BURMESE MARKET:
Shopping For Food

Vegetable market

In Burmese tradition, a housewife will wake up very early and go to the market carrying a plastic or cane basket to buy food for the day's cooking. Early visits are essential to make the best selection from the goods the market has to offer. This traditional approach continues today as refrigerators are expensive and can only be afforded by the wealthier members of the community.

Markets are not normally under a single roof, but are more likely to extend over a wider area into the nearby streets. Individual street stalls are also common but most people will go to the market for their day's shopping.

One food market was about fifteen minutes walking distance from our home. Occasionally I would go there with my mother before breakfast. My mother liked to go to the section where live chickens were kept in cages. She would select a plump chicken and it was tagged on one leg with a number. The same number tag was handed to my mother so she could claim her chicken later. Then, while we continued to shop or have breakfast, our chicken would be killed, plucked, and cleaned.

Many Burmese avoid eating meat from four-legged animals as they consider animals such as cows and pigs to have human-like characteristics. As we would more easily talk to a horse or a cow, it is easy to understand the view that these animals are spiritually linked to mankind.

In Burma, Buddhists consider it more sinful to kill four-legged animals (cows, pigs) than two-legged ones (chickens, ducks). Least sinful is killing creatures with no legs at all. Eating sea creatures such as fish or prawns is therefore less sinful than chicken, which, in turn, is less sinful than pork. In contrast, people from the Chinese community are less concerned with this practice and consume large quantities of pork.

Prawn at market

Fish is abundant in Burma along the coastal areas. In the markets, there are many fish stalls. Each stall will specialize in one or two types of fresh fish and hold just enough stock for the day. Another part of the market is devoted to dried foodstuffs. There you will find dried, salted fish for sale. Whether fresh or dried, the price of fish is relatively cheap compared to meat or poultry.

There are many varieties of fish sold, including anabas, carp, catfish, cuttlefish, eel, featherback, kingfish, ladyfish, mackerel, perch, pomfret, sardine, shad, snapper, squid, tuna, and butterfish. Other seafood, such as fresh prawns and shrimp are also available. Both range in size and can be very tasty. Three large king prawns could weigh about 12 ounces! While shrimp are relatively cheap, prawns are the most expensive and can only be afforded by wealthy people. Dried shrimp are also used widely in soups, dips, or fried vegetables.

In another section of the market, many types of vegetables are grouped together on the ground. In this area, one walks along a narrow footpath between these vegetables to choose and buy the best selection at the best prices. Types of vegetables include snake beans, eggplant, cauliflower, cabbage, gourd, Chinese green vegetables, watercress, bean sprouts, parsley, cucumber, ladyfingers, roselle

Banana trunk

leaves, tomatoes, snow-pea leaves, ash pumpkin, asparagus, bamboo shoots, basil, beans, beetroot, bell pepper, carrot, celery, chayote, leek, lettuce, loofah, mint, mushroom, okra, radish, string bean, potato, corns, taro, limes, and fresh tamarind. One of the most important vegetables available is the banana trunk (Ngat-Byor-Ou). This is used to cook one of the most authentic and popular breakfast treats, Rice Noodles with Fish Gravy (Mok-Hin-Kar; page 198).

Other market stores sell ginger, onions, garlic and potatoes. Some stalls sell tofu and bean sprouts. Bean sprouts are splashed with water occasionally to keep them moist and looking fresh.

Chilies at market

At the spice section, different types of spices are displayed inside big plastic bags for buyers to select the amount that they want. When you buy it, the spice is put into a cone-shaped carrier made of paper. This is then tucked in neatly for the customer to bring home.

Another section of the market is for chilies and paprika. Fresh and semi-dried chilies are available; their shapes range from long to short and from round to thin, while their color and taste also vary.

Rice is also sold in the markets. There are different types of rice with different flavors, shapes, and textures. Rice is kept in big bamboo or cane containers. Good quality rice is expensive and eaten by middle- to upper-class people, while lower quality rice is the cheapest and is eaten by lower-class or poor people.

Fruits are abundant according to the season. Seasonal fruits include orange, pear, mango, banana, pomegranate, durian, palmyra, pineapple, apple, jackfruit, water melon, guava, rambutan, jujube, avocado pear, lychee, custard apple, plum, grape, papaya, and peach. Berries such as strawberry and gooseberry are also on sale. Most fruits are grown in upper Burma where the weather is cooler.

Many stalls sell breakfasts of white rice, glutinous rice, bread, pancakes, and noodle soup. Tea and coffee are also popular and very common. Two types of freshly brewed tea are served, the traditional Burmese tea and the Western style with milk and sugar. I was fortunate that some of these breakfast stalls were located outside my house. Each morning we would ask for money from our mother and choose our preferred tasty treat for breakfast. Two of my favorites were Rice Noodle with Fish Gravy (page 198) and Coconut Chicken Noodle Soup (page 195). They are also made at home for special occasions such as birthdays, weddings, parties, or special family gatherings. Family members and friends often participate in cooking these national dishes having friendly conversations while they are being prepared. It is a happy occasion where everyone catches up with each other and looks forward to their meal.

In Burma, many people buy these special soups from food stalls in the market. Unfortunately, in Australia, we do not have such takeaway shops where we can go and eat daily. So we have to cook these soups at home ourselves; usually I cook them when I have the craving and the spare time, during the weekend. I always cook in a three-gallon pot from which we eat the whole day. Usually, my mother, sister, or friends assist me in cooking while chitchatting and listening to music. These special dishes take time to prepare but when they are cooked, family members and friends enjoy them and we all have a good time.

BURMESE KITCHEN

The Burmese Kitchen is relatively simple with few utensils and little furniture. A common kitchen would contain the following cooking equipment.

Basic Kitchen Utensils

Stove

A common Burmese custom, particularly in urban areas, is to use a small aluminum pot that burns kerosene. The lid has holes for twisted thick threads or white ropes, which are burned at the lid like a wick. These dangle down into the pot where they are soaked in a pool of kerosene. One danger with this type of stove is that it can easily explode and start a fire. A more recent innovation is to use a clay pot powered by electricity. In country areas, wood or charcoal is still used for cooking.

Table for the stove

The cooking pot is usually placed on a table or concrete block because it is easier to prepare and cook while standing. In the traditional approach, used in country areas, the stove is placed on the ground. One must kneel down in order to do the cooking.

Kitchen table

A small wooden table is used to prepare vegetables, meat, and other food. This table is usually quite low as the Burmese prefer to sit on the floor, wearing the traditional longyi, when preparing food. This garment allows the wearer to sit on the floor quite comfortably with legs crossed or folded.

Kitchen cupboard

This is a wooden cabinet with mesh screen to allow air to circulate. Cooked foods are kept here to avoid flies or cockroaches. I recall my mother also placed a bowl of water under each of leg to stop ants from crawling up the cupboard. I can remember seeing little dead ants in the bowl and assumed they drowned in their search for food.

Rice pot

A small aluminum pot is used for cooking rice. For those who can afford it, an electric rice cooker is a popular alternative.

Aluminum or tin pot

Aluminum pots are also used for cooking meat, poultry, or making soup. Most households will have a set of pots with thin flat lids. These are of various different sizes and are usually stacked inside each other when not in use.

Clay pot

A small clay pot is available in almost every Burmese kitchen. It is not used for cooking but designed to ferment the fish or make Burmese fish sauce (known as *nga-pi-yae*).

Aluminum or tin kettle

A Burmese kettle is more like a jug or similar container. It has a lid and a handle as well as a spout for pouring. Material is usually aluminum or tin. It is used to boil water.

Burmese water vase

An earthenware vase is used to store drinking water. A cup is usually left on the lid for shared use. This Burmese style of refrigeration keeps water very cool naturally.

Plate or bowl shelf

These days, a tiered plastic rack from Thailand or China, is used to store washed plates and bowls. Sometimes a small bowl is used to keep spoons together.

FLAVORS OF BURMA

Mortar and pestle

The mortar and pestle is an essential tool for pounding popular ingredients such as onions, garlic, chilies, and ginger. Both parts are round and made from some form of heavy stone. Pounding noises can be heard in the neighborhood every morning or afternoon signifying that someone is preparing their family's meal.

Other apparatus

Other equipment includes thick wooden chopping board, chopper, and small knives. A round bamboo tray is also used to shake, rotate, and toss rice and lentils. This is done to find and discard dirt, tiny stones, or similar impurities.

Burmese Measurements: Bait-Dar-Kyat-Thar

The weight measurement in Burma is not pounds or kilograms but "viss." One viss is about 3.6 pounds or 1.6 kilograms. Like most modern measurements, a viss is divided into a hundred ticals. In the Burmese language, the word for viss is pronounced "Bait-Dar" and the word for tical is pronounced "Kyat-Thar." As shopkeepers use scales with a standard set of weights, shopping is done in convenient multiples of 10, 20, or 50 ticals. One or two viss would be ample to carry.

Commonly Used Ingredients

Almost every Burmese kitchen uses a basic set of common, non-perishable ingredients like salts and spices. As most people are paid monthly, it is much easier for them to plan ahead and buy enough basic ingredients to last for the whole month. Buying these nonperishable foods in bulk also significantly reduces the food bill.

With little refrigeration, perishable foods like meat, poultry, seafood, and vegetables have to be bought daily. This means that all regular meals are prepared with the freshest of ingredients.

The following are the most common basic ingredients found in a Burmese kitchen. These are stored for the month and used in almost every Burmese dish.

Ingredients	Characteristics
Chili	Comes in a variety of shapes, sizes, and degrees of spiciness (hot or mild). Used to add reddish color and hot taste to the dish.
Curry powder	Provides color, flavor, and fragrance. Usually prepared and sold by Indian people or homemade in Burma. Made from ingredients such as cumin, cinnamon, cardamom, clove, coriander, peppercorn, and bay leaves, which are roasted and pounded for cooking.
Dried shrimp	Usually pounded using a mortar and pestle. Often an added ingredient when preparing salads, soups, or fried dishes.
Fish sauce	Adds salty taste and unique flavor. Made in Burma from fermented fish.
Garlic	Burmese garlic is small and reddish. This is an essential ingredient to add flavor and overcome meat odor.

Ginger	Overcomes fish or meat odor. Only fresh ginger is used in Burmese cooking. I think the readymade powder is no match for the flavor of the freshly pounded and squeezed ginger juice for marinating.
Lemon/lime	Provides the well-known sour but refreshing tastes.
Onion	Used for any cooking and a must for all curries and salads. Burmese onions are usually quite small. Both red and white are used to add flavor and sweetness.
Rice	White rice is grown in Burma. Different prices prevail depending on quality and seasonal availability.
Salt	Common basic ingredient.
Shrimp/fish paste	Provides salty taste and strong fragrance. Some pastes are used to add darker color to the dish.
Sweet paprika	Reddish spice that adds color and flavor to most dishes, especially curry dishes.
Tamarind	Dried tamarind is soaked in warm water then squeezed to extract the juice. Gives a sour taste and adds brown color to the dish.
Turmeric powder	Adds taste and color to the dishes. This yellow powder usually gives a golden appearance to a variety of dishes.

Burmese Curry (Sepyan) Cooking Processes

Burmese cooking involves a few basic steps familiar to almost everybody. Typically, the preparation starts by soaking and pounding some of the basic ingredients. This is done manually using the mortar and pestle. Usually, meat, poultry, and fish are marinated before cooking.

This process, if followed properly, will produce the thickening sauce and mouthwatering appearance that are characteristic of many Burmese dishes.

Step	Process
Pounding the ingredients (e.g. chili, onion, garlic, etc.)	Chilies are soaked in a bowl of warm water for about 10 minutes to soften them before pounding. Usually a pinch of salt is added to the chilies during pounding. Onions and garlic are added. Ginger is pounded thoroughly so that the juice will overcome any meat or fish odor.
Marinating the meat or fish	Meat and fish are marinated using the pounded ingredients to capture the fragrance. This is best done well in advance of cooking. Fish sauce, salt, turmeric powder, sweet paprika, and curry powder can also be added. For better results, use your hand to mix the ingredients.
Heating the oil and sautéing the ingredients	The saucepan or frying pan must be dry before pouring the oil. Heat must be low to medium when the pounded ingredients are added. They are then sautéed slowly to provide a thickening sauce. Care should be taken to ensure the mixture is not burned. Burmese people use a generous amount of oil for cooking.
Sautéing the meat or fish	Meat or fish is added to the sautéed ingredients on a medium heat. Blend well so the aroma, color, and texture of the pounded ingredients can be fully absorbed into the main dish.

Adding water or stock   Chicken stock or water is then added a little at a time. Add just enough to cover the meat or fish. Cover and cook on medium heat. Bring to a boil and allow the dish to simmer slowly until it is tender. With meat, more time should be taken and more water added as required.

Forming a clear oily sauce   When the dish is almost cooked, remove the lid and reduce to a low heat. This will boil off any excess water and leave a layer of clear oil rising above the sauce. You now have the authentic curry sauce known as Sepyan.

Burmese Menu

A typical Burmese menu will consist of a main meal, rice, and a number of other dishes. Unlike other cooking styles that have an entrée before a main meal, all Burmese dishes are served together and eaten at the same time.

Rice	Rice is the staple food of Burma. It is usually boiled or steamed but it can be cooked in a more exotic manner to add extra fragrance.
Curry (Sepyan)	This is the main dish that accompanies the rice. It is usually cooked in the sepyan style, with the thickening sauce described above. Burmese dishes are of two main types: with or without the Indian-style curry powder.
Steamed/sour dishes	Steamed seafood dishes can also accompany the rice. Sour dishes are also common. These usually use tamarind or tomatoes as a base.
Salad	The authentic way to mix Burmese salads is by hand. Cooked meat, seafood or raw vegetables are mixed with fish sauce, chili powder, finely sliced onions (both raw and fried) and fried garlic. Lemon or lime juice is also added.
Stir-fry	This is a common dish anywhere in Asia. It consists of simple, quick stir-fried meat or vegetable to provide alternative tastes to the other dishes.
Raw or boiled vegetable (side dish)	Vegetable side dishes may be cooked or raw. When cooked, quick boiling is much preferred to steaming. Common boiled vegetables include eggplant, cabbage, and gourd. Raw vegetables are made with lime leaves, lettuce, radishes, and cucumbers. These vegetables are always served with many

types of dips or more simply with fish sauce.

Dip (side dish) Dips, which can be a pounded paste or thick sauce, are extremely appetizing when served with vegetables.

(a) Pounded pastes, some of which are very hot and salty, are very much an acquired taste and must be used sparingly. They are made from dried shrimp, fish paste, garlic, and chilies. Ingredients are usually roasted and pounded together using the mortar and pestle.

(b) Thick sauce can be made from either fermented fish or vegetables such as tomato cooked with garlic, onions, and chilies. One fermented fish sauce (*nga-pi-yae*) is so popular that it is generally served free, as a dip, in Burmese restaurants.

Soup Soup stock is made from chicken, pork, or seafood such as grilled fish or dried shrimp. Usually vegetables are added just before serving. Plain or clear soups can balance the strong taste of other dishes. With simple ingredients, they are economical and easy to prepare. More elaborate soups use extra ingredients to provide exotic taste and flavors.

Meals and Serving Customs

There are three main meals per day in Burma. Breakfast is usually very simple. It could be the previous night's leftover rice that is simply fried with some peas, onions, and eggs. Otherwise some fried fritters accompany the plain rice or the fried rice. It is more common to eat out as there are a variety of food stalls which sell various breakfast treats. Tea houses are very common in Burma. They are regarded as the meeting places for most people. Burmese people love tea and coffee. This is usually accompanied by fresh oven-baked *naan*, a piece of sweet dough that is heated in a hot concrete charcoal oven.

Lunch generally includes rice, a curry dish, salad, and soup. One point worth noting is that Burmese meals do not have any entrée. Dinner, which includes rice and most typical dishes, is usually followed by seasonal fruits such as mango, jackfruit, or rumbutung.

Later in the night, Burmese Tea, Burmese Tea Salad (page 191) and Burmese sweets such as palm sugar are usually served.

Traditionally, Burmese food is served at a round and low table. The Burmese custom is to sit on the floor. The table is low enough to rest one's elbows. People gather around the table and sit comfortably on a mat with all the dishes within arm's length. Males sit comfortably with their legs crossed while females fold their legs and tuck their feet to the side. The custom is that a finger bowl and tea towel are provided at the table for anyone to wash their hands.

In the traditional way of eating, Burmese will use the tips of their five fingers to bring food to their mouth in a neat way. Typical dishes include rice, curries, salads, vegetables, and side dishes. Side dishes are usually cucumber, and tomato slices, which are eaten with the Burmese traditional fermented fish sauce, *nga-pi-yae* or Fried Shrimp with Shrimp Paste (page 146).

Serving Quantity

Please note that recipes in this cookbook serve 2 (very generously) to 4 people most. Also note that usually 3 to 4 dishes are cooked to serve with rice and so it is possible to serve 5 or 6 people. It is the Burmese custom to share food with other people and hence if there are more people, eat less so that everyone has a share of each dish.

The special occasion dishes can be serve 8 to 10 people. Usually, these dishes can be eaten at more than one meal.

VARIOUS COOKING METHODS FOR RICE

VARIOUS COOKING METHODS FOR RICE

In the past, Burma was one of the leading rice producers of the world. The heavy monsoon rain from upper Burma brings down the fertile soil to the valleys and coastal plains in lower Burma.

Burma is blessed with the Irrawaddy River, which flows into a delta, west of Rangoon. Farmers live and grow rice along the delta, the river valleys and coastal plains. The hot, wet climates of these places are perfect conditions for rice production.

Rice to the Burmese is as important as pasta to Italians or bread to the Westerners. There are different kinds of rice grown in Burma and each has a different shape, taste, texture, and aroma.

COOKING RICE THE BURMESE WAY

Burmese people boil rice in a pot and then discard the water. The rice continues to simmer on low heat until it is fully cooked. Typically, in the West, rice is boiled, then steamed until cooked. Water is not usually discarded. The Burmese approach of removing the starch from the rice is good for diabetics as well as for dietary purposes.

Ingredients
2 cups white rice

Method
- Soak rice with enough water to cover in a pot for about 15 minutes. Wash and drain.
- Add 7 cups water to cover rice and boil over medium heat for 15 to 20 minutes.
- Pour off excess water and drain rice in a strainer.
- Return rice to the pot, cover with lid, and simmer over low heat for 15 to 20 minutes until rice is fully cooked.

Makes 4 servings.

RED LENTIL AND BUTTER RICE

To get the best results, use Indian long-grain basmati rice or Sri Lankan short and round samba rice, which makes for fluffy rice. Red lentils could be preboiled until half-cooked, if they require precooking. Otherwise, add them immediately after the rice is boiled and simmer together with the rice until fully cooked. Butter and spices added to this dish produce a fragrant buttery rice.

Ingredients

¼ cup dried red lentils
2 tablespoons butter
2 teaspoons oil
1 small onion, cut into 4 pieces
2 bay leaves
10 cloves
1 cinnamon stick
10 cardamom pods
2 cups rice, washed and drained
1 teaspoon sugar
½ teaspoon salt

Method

- Soak the red lentils in warm water for about 2 hours. Wash and drain.
- In a rice cooker, add butter, oil, and onions and fry for 1 minute.
- Add bay leaves, cloves, cinnamon, and cardamoms and fry for 1 minute.
- Add rice, sugar, and salt and stir for 1 minute until the rice is fragrant.
- Add 2 cups water and stir well. Cover and cook the rice according to manufacturer's directions.
- Once the rice is cooked, add lentils and stir well with the rice. Continue to simmer for 30 to 45 minutes on "warm" setting until rice and lentils are fully cooked.

To Serve: Red Lentil and Butter Rice can be accompanied by any of the curry dishes, salad dishes, dips, and soups.

Makes 4 to 6 servings.

COCONUT RICE

This rice is cooked during special occasions to substitute for plain boiled rice. Coconut adds a beautiful fragrance as well as a creamy taste.

In Western countries, we have the convenience of using a rice cooker and canned coconut milk or coconut cream, making this dish very simple and easy to prepare. In Burma, however, most people prefer to use fresh coconuts.

Ingredients
2 cups short-grain rice
4 teaspoons white sugar
1 teaspoon salt
2 medium onions, quartered
1 small can (4 ounces)
    coconut cream

Method
- Wash rice and drain well.
- Add rice, sugar, salt, onion pieces, and water to the rice cooker until the water level reaches the number of rice cups to be cooked (e.g. Level 2 for 2 cups).
- Add coconut cream and stir well. Cover to cook the rice, according to manufacturer's instructions.
- When the rice cooker switches from "cook" to "warm" setting, stir rice with a spatula.
- Simmer rice for 20 minutes.

To Serve: Coconut rice is usually accompanied by curry dishes, especially Curry Chicken with Potatoes and Lemongrass (page 86), and Lemon and Onion Salad (page 113).

Makes 4 servings.

GOLDEN GLUTINOUS RICE

The glutinous rice gets its golden appearance and nice fragrance from the turmeric powder. In Burma, this glutinous rice is considered a breakfast treat. In market stalls, it is served on banana leaves. I love the crunchy top layer of the glutinous rice baked in the oven. Usually it is served with a mixture of freshly grated coconut, roasted sesame seeds, and salt.

This dish is not suitable for a rice cooker. Use a nonstick frying pan or wok.

Ingredients
2 cups glutinous rice
4½ tablespoons oil
1 small onion, finely sliced
1 teaspoon turmeric powder

Garnish
¼ cup sesame seeds
2 teaspoons salt
1 fresh coconut, grated

Method
- Soak the glutinous rice in water overnight. Wash and drain 30 minutes before cooking.
- Heat oil in a nonstick saucepan or wok. Add onions and fry over low-medium heat for about 3 minutes.
- Add rice and turmeric powder. Fry over low-medium heat for about 3 minutes.
- Add 2¾ cups water and mix together. Cover and cook over low-medium heat for about 20 minutes, until rice is well cooked and water is totally absorbed.
- Scoop all the cooked rice in a baking dish and pat out evenly. Brown the rice at 400°F (200°C) for about 25 minutes, or until the top part of the rice is golden brown and crispy.

- While the rice is baking, dry-fry the sesame seeds and salt in a nonstick frying pan for about 5 minutes or until sesame seeds are golden brown.
- Remove the sesame seeds and salt mixture. Pound using a mortar and pestle (or blend using a blender).

To Serve: Scoop 3 to 4 tablespoons of golden glutinous rice onto a small plate. Serve with a pinch of the roasted and pounded sesame and salt mixture and 1 tablespoon of grated coconut flesh.

Other accompaniments such as boiled green peas, crispy fried onions, pounded dried shrimp, fried fish, or Fried Shrimp with Shrimp Paste (page 146) add extra taste to this breakfast treat.

Makes 4 servings.

CURRY DISHES WITHOUT USING CURRY POWDER: SEPYAN

CURRY DISHES WITHOUT USING CURRY POWDER: SEPYAN

As explained in the Burmese Curry Cooking Processes section (page 44), *sepyan* refers to any dish where the excess water is boiled away, leaving only a layer of oil above the gravy sauce to give that authentic characteristic to the Burmese dish.

Burma has hot weather and typically, hot dishes accompany the rice. These hot dishes stimulate the body and allow it to sweat and cool down. Curry dishes are influenced by India, but the Burmese use fewer spices and ingredients. Therefore, some dishes may look like a curry dish but could contain little or no spices or curry powder.

Burmese people use simple ingredients such as onion, garlic, and chilies that can be found in the kitchen and so these dishes are easy to prepare. This method, without any curry powder, creates an alternative taste for those who cannot tolerate strong spices.

The best way to prepare the *sepyan* dish is to pound chilies, ginger, garlic, and onions using a mortar and pestle and marinate well with the accompanying meat (for better results, use the hand to marinade). This is the traditional way of pounding and marinating the meat, but be careful not to get the ingredients into your eyes. Otherwise, use a blender to blend the ingredients, but do not overblend them as the onions could become too watery. Alternatively, chop or dice everything on a chopping board using a Chinese chopper.

DOUBLE-FRIED FISH CURRY

Fish is abundant in Burma and relatively cheap compared to meat or poultry. This recipe is simple to cook but it is delicious.

The fish used for this recipe is usually butterfish or carp and both are delicious. Spanish mackerel or kingfish could be substituted.

Marinade
½ teaspoon salt
1 large piece (1 inch) fresh ginger, blended or pounded to make juice
3 cloves garlic, blended
1 teaspoon turmeric powder

Ingredients
2 pieces (1 pound) butterfish, Spanish mackerel, or king fish fillets
2 medium tomatoes
5½ tablespoons oil
1 large onion, finely chopped
2 teaspoons sweet paprika
4 teaspoons fish sauce
3 to 4 fresh chilies

Method
- Marinate fish fillets and let them stand for about 15 minutes.
- Slice 1 tomato finely. Slice the other into wedges.
- Heat oil in a frying pan. Add marinated fish fillets and fry over medium heat for 3 to 5 minutes on each side or until fish is cooked. Remove fish fillets and drain.
- Add onions to the frying pan and sauté over medium heat for about 5 minutes or until the onions are transparent.
- Add thinly sliced tomatoes and paprika, fry over medium heat for about 4 minutes or until tomatoes are all dissolved.
- Add fish sauce and ⅘ cup water, cover and cook over low heat for 2 minutes.

Continued

- Return the fried fish fillets to the frying pan and simmer over low heat for 6 to 8 minutes. Continue to simmer until sauce is reduced, leaving the thick tomato and onion sauce and a clear oily layer on the top of the dish.
- Garnish with fresh chilies and tomato wedges.

To Serve: Serve with plain boiled rice.

Makes 4 servings.

CHICKEN CURRY WITH GRAVY SAUCE

Chicken has always been expensive in Burma, as I could remember twenty years ago, and it still is. Burmese people consider themselves privileged to eat chicken. They will show off to their neighbors that they are cooking fried chicken or chicken curry. They are very proud of the fact that they can afford to buy chicken as it is considered a wealthy or upper class dish.

As a sign of respect, the heart of the chicken is usually offered to elderly people. Lovers offer the chicken heart to their loved one to symbolize their love.

I love using curry leaves when I cook curry dishes because of the beautiful fragrance that they give out; one can smell the aroma from afar. I recommend adding a few of these leaves to the Chicken Curry dishes in particular.

Ingredients

1½ to 2 pounds chicken wings (about 7 to 10 pieces)	5 cloves garlic
	2 large and long red chilies
	4 teaspoons fish sauce
1 small piece (¼ inch) fresh ginger	½ teaspoon salt
	¼ teaspoon turmeric powder
2 to 3 medium onions, quartered	1 teaspoon sweet paprika
	4 tablespoons oil
	3 curry leaves (optional)

Method

- Cut the chicken wing from the joint. Wash each piece and drain well.
- In a blender, combine ginger, onions, garlic, and chilies and blend until smooth.

Continued

- Combine fish sauce, salt, turmeric, paprika, oil, and the onion mixture in a bowl. Add chicken to the marinade and let stand for about 15 minutes. To produce a thicker gravy sauce, use the hand to marinate the chicken for 2 minutes.
- Pour chicken in a saucepan and brown well over medium heat for 15 minutes until you can smell the nice aroma of the chicken.
- Add 1 cup water to cover the chicken pieces and cover and bring to a boil. Reduce to medium heat and cook for 20 minutes or until the chicken is thoroughly cooked.
- Uncover and cook for 5 minutes over low heat until most of the water is evaporated. Stir the chicken mixture occasionally to avoid burning.

To Serve: Serve with plain boiled rice.

Makes 4 servings.

CURRY CHICKEN WITH GOURD IN THIN SAUCE

This is a popular chicken dish in the country area. It is quite a hot dish because a lot of fresh chilies are used. This dish will not produce a thick gravy sauce but rather a more diluted sauce. This could be served as sweet and hot chili chicken soup.

A type of melon called calabash gourd adds extra sweetness to this dish. This is a very popular melon in Burma, as it can be cooked in several different ways. It can be fried in batter, cooked with meat or prawns or made into soup. Look for gourd in Thai, Vietnamese, Chinese, or even in Western grocery stores.

Marinade
2 tablespoons fish sauce
½ teaspoon turmeric powder
½ teaspoon sweet paprika
1½ teaspoons salt

Ingredients
1 small chicken (2 pounds)
1 big onion, quartered
4 cloves garlic
1 small piece (¼ inch) fresh ginger
5 to 8 fresh long chilies
4½ tablespoons oil
1 pound gourd, cut into 1-inch slices

Method

- Wash and chop the chicken into medium pieces. Marinate chicken with fish sauce, turmeric, paprika, and salt and let stand for 15 minutes.
- In a blender, combine onions, garlic, ginger, and chilies and blend well.
- Heat oil in a medium saucepan or a pot. Add onion mixture and sauté slowly over medium heat for 5 to 8 minutes.

Continued

- Add chicken pieces with marinade and cook well over medium to high heat for 7 minutes.
- Add gourd pieces and stir well for about 5 minutes over medium heat.
- Add $2\frac{1}{2}$ cups water to the chicken and gourd mixture, cover, and bring to boil. Reduce to low to medium heat and continue to cook for about 30 minutes or until the gourd pieces are tender.

To Serve: Serve with plain boiled rice and enjoy the hot chicken liquid as well.

Makes 4 servings.

Coconut milk gives this dish a rather sweet taste and the fried onions provide a nice fragrance. This dish would definitely suit Western taste buds.

Ingredients

1 small chicken (2 pounds)
3 medium onions
1 small piece (¼ inch) fresh ginger, pounded or blended
3 cloves garlic, pounded or blended
3 fresh chilies, pounded or blended
4 tablespoons oil
½ teaspoon turmeric powder
½ teaspoon sweet paprika
2 teaspoons fish sauce
1 small can (4 ounces) coconut milk
½ teaspoon salt

Method

- Wash the chicken and chop into small pieces.
- Slice 1 onion finely. In a blender, combine ginger, 2 reserved onions, garlic, and chilies and blend well.
- Heat oil in a medium saucepan or pot. Add sliced onion and turmeric powder and fry for about 3 minutes over medium heat until golden brown. Remove onion from oil.
- Add blended garlic mixture to the oil in the same saucepan or pot and fry for about 2 minutes over medium heat.
- Add chicken pieces, paprika, and fish sauce and stir well for about 8 minutes until chicken pieces are quite brown.
- Add coconut milk and 1 can water and bring to a boil.
- Return the fried onions to the pan, add salt and simmer on low heat for about 30 minutes, stirring occasionally.

To Serve: Serve with plain boiled rice.

Makes 4 servings.

BEEF CURRY WITH FISH PASTE

The fish paste adds a distinctive taste and browning effect, while the tomatoes add a slightly sour taste to this dish. Together, these combinations make quite an interesting and pleasant alternative to the usual curry dish.

Ingredients

- ½ pound top side beef
- 1 medium piece (½ inch) fresh ginger, blended or pounded to make juice
- ¼ teaspoon salt
- 4 tablespoons oil
- 2 medium onions, chopped or blended
- 3 cloves garlic, chopped or blended
- 2 small soft tomatoes, sliced finely
- 1 teaspoon sweet paprika
- 1 slice fish paste (⅛ inch)
- 3 to 4 fresh chilies
- 2 stems fresh Chinese parsley

Method

- Wash and cut beef into small ½-inch cubes. Marinate in ginger juice and salt and let stand for 15 minutes.
- Dissolve fish paste in 1 tablespoon warm water.
- Heat oil in a pot. Add onions and garlic and sauté over medium heat for 4 minutes.
- Add tomatoes, paprika, and fish paste solution and cook for about 5 minutes until the tomatoes are cooked thoroughly.
- Add beef cubes and stir for about 5 minutes or until the beef turns brown and water from the beef is absorbed.
- Add ⅓ cup water to the beef and bring to a boil. Reduce to low-medium heat, cover and cook for about 5 minutes or until the beef is cooked.
- Add fresh chilies and parsley and simmer for 1 minute.

To Serve: Serve with plain boiled rice.

Makes 4 servings.

PRAWN CURRY

In Burma, prawns were quite cheap about twenty years ago. I fondly remember those tiger prawns turning a wonderful pink-orange color when fried in hot oil. Burmese tiger prawns are very big. In fact, they are about twice the size of the largest tiger or king prawn in Western countries. These days, however, the prawn prices have soared as most of them are exported. Prawns are now almost inaccessible to Burmese people with an average budget.

These prawns cooked with tomatoes and some spices create a mouthwatering dish. Your friends or dinner guests will surely be impressed by this delicious curry.

Ingredients

¼ pound king prawns or medium-size prawns
1 teaspoon fish sauce
½ teaspoon salt
5 cloves garlic
1 small piece (¼ inch) fresh ginger (optional)
1 medium onion, quartered
3 to 4 small chilies or 2 long chilies
5 tablespoons oil
1 small ripe tomato, cut into small pieces
½ teaspoon sweet paprika
¼ teaspoon turmeric powder

Method

- Devein the prawns and remove the heads. Marinate prawns in fish sauce and salt.
- In a blender, combine garlic, ginger, onion quarters, and chilies. Blend until smooth.
- Heat oil in a saucepan. Add onion mixture and sauté over medium heat for 8 to 10 minutes or until the onion is transparent.
- Add tomato pieces and fry for about 5 minutes over medium heat or until the tomatoes are cooked thoroughly.

Continued

- Add paprika and turmeric powder and stir quickly for about 30 seconds.
- Add ½ cup water and mix well for about 1 minute over medium heat. If the sauce is quite thick, add ¼ cup water and boil for 1 minute.
- Add prawns and stir well over high heat for about 3 minutes until the prawns curl into a circular shape and turn pink.
- Reduce to low heat and cook further for 5 minutes or until the sauce is reduced, leaving only the tomato gravy behind.

To Serve: Serve with plain boiled rice, or Red Lentil and Butter Rice (page 52), or Coconut Rice (page 53).

Makes 4 servings.

PORK CURRY WITH TAMARIND

Pork is a popular meat in Burma. It is relatively expensive but there are many parts of the pig that one can buy for cooking. Pig is a most beneficial and useful animal in that almost every part of it can be used for eating. Even the pig's hair is used to make hard bristle brush that is good for cleaning dirty wooden floors.

For the following recipe, it is best to use the three-layered pork. This is the pork belly portion with the meat on the bottom layer, fat in the middle layer and pork skin on the top layer. Although pork is quite fat, it is very tasty when cooked as a *sepyan* dish. Pork pieces should be cut in such a way that each piece retains all three layers.

The fatty part of the pork makes the dish very creamy and rich. Tamarind sauce is added to the dish to offset the rich taste of the curry pork. This adds a slightly sour taste to this delicious *sepyan* dish.

Ingredients	Marinade
1 tablespoon dried tamarind	4 teaspoons fish sauce
1 pound 3-layered pork belly	½ teaspoon turmeric powder
2½ tablespoons oil	1 small piece (¼ inch) fresh ginger, blended
	½ teaspoon salt
	4 cloves garlic, blended
	2 medium onions, blended
	1 teaspoon sweet paprika
	3 to 4 fresh chilies, blended

Method

- Soak the tamarind in a ¼ cup of warm water for about 15 minutes. Squeeze or press tamarind to get the juice and mix well with the water.

Continued

- Wash and chop the pork into 1-inch pieces. Marinate with the marinade ingredients and let stand for about 15 minutes.
- In a medium saucepan, add the marinated pork and oil. Cook over high heat for 4 minutes.
- Reduce to medium heat and cook for 5 minutes until the pork and the skin are very brown.
- Add 2 cups water, cover and bring to a boil. Reduce heat and simmer for 25 minutes or until the pork is very tender. If the meat is still tough, add 1/4 cup water and continue to simmer for 10 to 15 minutes or until pork is tender.
- When the meat is tender, reduce to low heat, add 2 tablespoons tamarind juice, and stir well. If extra sour taste is desired, add 1 more tablespoon tamarind juice and simmer for 2 minutes.

To Serve: Serve with plain boiled rice.

Makes 4 servings.

EGG CURRY WITH DRIED SHRIMP

I love eating eggs and this is one of my favorite egg dishes. It cooks so well with tomatoes and is a must to try for egg lovers. I have provided two options for cooking the eggs: scorched or unscorched. I prefer scorched eggs as they smell delicious and the crispy egg whites taste so good.

Ingredients

1 tablespoon dried tamarind

6 large eggs, hard boiled and shells removed

2½ tablespoons oil

2 medium onions, blended

3 cloves garlic, blended

2 fresh chilies

2 medium ripe tomatoes, cut into wedges

2 tablespoons dried shrimps, pounded or blended

1 teaspoon sweet paprika

½ teaspoon turmeric powder

4 teaspoons fish sauce

Parsley for garnish

Method

- Soak the tamarind in a ¼ cup of warm water for about 15 minutes. Squeeze or press tamarind to get the juice and mix well with the water.

Option 1 (scorched eggs): If the eggs are to be fried, do not cut the eggs. Heat oil in a frying pan and add the eggs and scorch them over low heat for about 5 minutes. Turn eggs to different sides and continue to scorch them evenly. Remove eggs from the saucepan and drain on a paper towel.

- Add onions, garlic, and chilies and fry over medium heat for about 3 minutes until onions are transparent.

- Add tomatoes and dried shrimps and cook for 3 to 5 minutes or until the tomatoes are cooked thoroughly.

Continued

- Add paprika, turmeric powder, fish sauce, 2 tablespoons tamarind juice (do not put the tamarind pieces in), and ⅓ cup water and simmer over low heat for 3 to 5 minutes or until a nice tomato sauce is formed.
- Add the fried eggs and cook for 4 to 5 minutes. Adjust taste accordingly. Add a little more tamarind juice if a more sour taste if preferred. Garnish with parsley for added flavor.

Option 2 (unscorched eggs):
- Cut the eggs into halves.
- Add oil to the saucepan or wok.
- Add onions, garlic, and chilies and fry over medium heat for about 3 minutes until onions are transparent.
- Add tomatoes and dried shrimps and cook for 3 to 5 minutes or until the tomatoes are cooked thoroughly.
- Add paprika, turmeric powder, fish sauce, 2 tablespoons tamarind juice (do not put the tamarind pieces in), and ⅓ cup water and simmer over low heat for 3 to 5 minutes or until a nice tomato sauce is formed.
- Add the eggs to the saucepan with the egg yolks facing down the pan. When scooping the eggs out of the saucepan, be careful not to drop or separate the egg yolks from the egg whites. Garnish with parsley.

To Serve: Serve with plain boiled rice.

Makes 6 servings.

CURRY DISHES
WITH SPICES:
SEPYAN

CURRY DISHES WITH SPICES: SEPYAN

As mentioned previously, *sepyan* refers to any curry dish (with or without spices) where the excess water is boiled away to leave only the oily layer above the gravy sauce to give that authentic characteristic to the Burmese dish. The following recipes use curry powder and I will simply call them curry dishes.

Many Indian people live in Burma, especially in Rangoon. Curry powder is an influence from India. I remember going with my mother to the curry powder factory and bought some spices. There, the spices were particularly fragrant and fresh. In the markets, ready-made curry powder is sold in small packages.

Mixed Vegetable Curry

MIXED VEGETABLE CURRY

This curry dish can be made from almost any type of vegetables that you may desire. However, I will use common vegetables that combine color and flavor. This is a favorite dish for vegetarians who enjoy curry.

Ingredients

4 tablespoons oil
1 big onion, blended
3 cloves garlic, blended
3 medium potatoes, peeled and cut into 8 pieces each
1 large eggplant, cut the same size as the potatoes
1 to 1½ pounds gourd, cut the same size as the potatoes
2 small carrots, cut the same size as the potatoes
2½ tablespoons curry powder
½ teaspoon turmeric powder
1½ teaspoons sweet paprika
4 teaspoons fish sauce
1 slice (¼ inch) shrimp paste
¼ cup long beans, cut in halves
2 firm tomatoes, cut into wedges
1 teaspoon salt

Method

- Dissolve shrimp paste in 1 tablespoon warm water.
- Heat oil in a big wok or pot. Add onion and garlic and sauté over medium heat for 5 minutes.
- Add potatoes and fry over medium heat for 1 minute.
- Add eggplant, gourd, carrot, curry powder, turmeric powder, and paprika and fry over medium heat for 1 minute.
- Add fish sauce, shrimp paste solution, and 3½ cups water to cover the vegetables and boil over medium heat for about 20 minutes until the potatoes are almost soft.
- Add long beans and tomatoes and cover and cook for about 10 minutes over medium heat. Add salt to taste.

To Serve: Serve with plain boiled rice, or Red Lentil and Butter Rice (page 52), or Coconut Rice (page 53).
Makes 6 servings.

BEEF CURRY WITH COCONUT MILK

This technique is the traditional method of cooking beef in a saucepan or a pot. This is an excellent way to cook the beef to its best taste. The coconut adds extra-sweet flavor and creaminess to the dish. The best meat to use for this dish is gravy beef. Gravy beef is tough and needs to be cooked well (about 2 hours) to make it moist and tender.

Ingredients

2 pounds gravy beef	5½ tablespoons oil
2 tablespoons fish sauce	2 teaspoons sweet paprika
1 teaspoon salt	1 tablespoon curry powder
1 small piece (¼ inch)	½ teaspoon turmeric powder
fresh ginger, blended	¼ teaspoon black pepper
2 medium onions, quartered	1 small can coconut milk
5 cloves garlic	(4 ounces)

Method

- Wash beef and cut into 2-inch pieces. Marinate with fish sauce and salt and let stand for 15 minutes. In a blender combine ginger, onions, and garlic and blend well.
- Heat oil in a pot. Add onion mixture to the pot and sauté over low to medium heat for about 8 minutes or until the onions are transparent.
- Add paprika, curry powder, and turmeric powder and stir for 1 minute.
- Increase to medium heat and add beef cubes to pot and stir well for 7 to 10 minutes or until the beef turns brown and the water from the beef is evaporated.
- Add 1⅓ cups water and black pepper to beef. Cover and simmer on very low heat for about 1½ hours or until beef is tender, stirring occasionally.
- Add coconut milk and cook over low heat for 20 minutes.

To Serve: Serve with plain boiled rice.

Makes 4 servings.

BEEF CURRY WITH YOGURT

In this recipe, I use yogurt to tenderize the meat. I also make use of a pressure cooker instead of a normal cooking pot to reduce cooking time to 25 minutes. If a normal cooking pot is used then please follow the instructions on the previous recipe, Beef Curry with Coconut Milk (page 80). This is the recipe for those who do not like coconut. The yogurt adds a slightly sour taste to this dish.

Ingredients

2 pounds gravy beef
1 tablespoon fish sauce
½ teaspoon turmeric powder
2 teaspoons salt
¾ cup plain yogurt
1 small piece (¼ inch) fresh ginger
6 cloves garlic
3 medium red onions, quartered
1 tablespoon sweet paprika
2 teaspoons curry powder
4 tablespoons oil

Method

- Wash and cut beef into 2-inch pieces and place in the pressure cooker.
- In a blender, combine ginger, garlic, and onions and blend well. Marinate beef with all the ingredients for 15 minutes.
- Add 1 cup water to the pressure cooker.
- Cover the lid tightly and cook over medium heat for 25 minutes.

To Serve: Serve with plain boiled rice, or Red Lentil and Butter Rice (page 52), or Coconut Rice (page 53).

Makes 4 servings.

DUCK CURRY

Duck is quite fat because of its thick fat skin, therefore it is important to trim off the skin and fat before cooking. You should buy a 3-pound duck and expect it to lose much of this weight when trimming the fat. Also be warned that duck has a strong odor by nature and therefore, generous amount of ginger and spices are used to overcome this smell.

Duck skin is only kept for Chinese Peking duck because the skin is the best part when barbecued. Note that duck meat is not as tender as chicken and cooking time takes longer. For this reason, vinegar is added during marinating process to tenderize the meat.

Ducks are abundant in Burma and cheaper than chicken. Also, in Burma, duck is usually steamed and shredded into pieces, and served with egg noodles and garlic oil as one of the most popular Chinese dishes.

Ingredients
3 pounds duck	2 teaspoons white vinegar
5 cloves garlic	2 teaspoons sweet paprika
2 medium onions, quartered	4 teaspoons curry powder
1 large piece (1 inch) fresh ginger, sliced	½ teaspoon turmeric powder
4 teaspoons fish sauce	1½ tablespoons oil
	½ teaspoon salt

Method
- Wash and cut the duck into medium bite-size pieces.
- In a blender, combine garlic, onions, and ginger and blend well.

To prepare the marinade: Combine fish sauce, vinegar, paprika, curry powder, and turmeric.
- Add the duck pieces to the marinade for 30 minutes.
- Heat oil in a pot. Add onion mixture and cook for 5 minutes over low heat until onions are transparent.

- Add marinated duck and cook over high heat for 7 to 10 minutes or until brown.
- Add 4 cups water and cover and bring to boil over high heat.
- Reduce to medium heat and cook for about 40 minutes, stirring the mixture occasionally.
- Add salt and reduce to low heat and simmer for an additional 30 minutes or until duck meat is tender.

To Serve: Serve with plain boiled rice.

Makes 6 servings.

LAMB CURRY WITH SPLIT PEAS

This curry dish has probably been derived from an original Indian recipe. I certainly can see a strong Indian inheritance in the choice of ingredients such as lamb, peas, and spices. The split peas add creaminess and an extra sweet taste to this lamb dish. The split pea sauce is very delicious to eat with boiled rice.

Ingredients

¾ cup yellow split pea
1 pound lamb cubes (1 inch)
4 teaspoons white vinegar
Juice of ½ small lemon
1 medium piece (½ inch) fresh ginger, blended or pounded to make juice
2 medium onions, quartered
5 cloves garlic
1 fresh long chili
1 stalk lemongrass, white part only
4½ tablespoons oil
1 teaspoon turmeric powder
1 teaspoon sweet paprika
2 ½ teaspoons curry powder
4 teaspoons fish sauce
½ teaspoon salt

Method

- Soak the yellow split peas in water for at least 4 hours. Wash and drain.
- Marinate the lamb cubes with vinegar, lemon juice, and ginger for about 15 minutes.
- In a blender, combine onions, garlic, chili, and lemongrass and blend well.
- Heat oil in a saucepan. Add onion mixture and sauté for 5 to 8 minutes over low-medium heat until the onion is transparent.
- Add turmeric powder, paprika, and curry powder and continue to sauté for 1 minute.
- Add lamb pieces and cook well on medium heat for about 5 minutes until the meat turns brown.

- Add drained peas, fish sauce, 4 cups water, and salt and cook on medium heat for 20 to 30 minutes until lamb and peas are tender. Avoid stirring the lamb and pea mixture to prevent peas from breaking. Just hold the pot off the stove and shake it gently to prevent the meat and peas from getting burned while cooking.

To Serve: Serve with plain boiled rice, or Red Lentil and Butter Rice (page 52), or Coconut Rice (page 53).

Makes 4 servings.

CHICKEN CURRY WITH POTATOES AND LEMONGRASS

Lemongrass provides a unique flavor and fragrance to the chicken and potatoes in this curry dish. My mum makes the best chicken curry, while my father makes the best beef curry.

Ingredients

2 pounds chicken drumsticks
   or 2-pound chicken,
   cut into small pieces
1 tablespoon fish sauce
½ teaspoon turmeric powder
2 teaspoons sweet paprika
2 tablespoons curry powder
1 small piece (¼ inch)
   fresh ginger
3 cloves garlic
2 medium onions
3 to 4 fat chilies (optional)
4 tablespoon oil
3 stalks lemongrass,
   pounded and cut into
   4 pieces each
4 medium potatoes, cut
   into 4 pieces each
1 teaspoon salt

Method

- Wash chicken and dry. To prepare the marinade, combine the fish sauce, turmeric powder, paprika, and curry powder. Add the chicken to marinade and let stand for 20 minutes.
- In a blender, combine ginger, garlic, onions, and chilies and blend until smooth.
- Heat oil in a saucepan. Add lemongrass and onion mixture and fry for about 8 minutes on medium heat.
- Pour in chicken pieces with marinade and cook over medium heat, stirring well, for about 5 minutes or until the chicken is almost cooked.

- Add potatoes and salt and stir for about 3 minutes.
- Add 2½ cups water to cover the chicken and potatoes. Boil on medium heat with the lid on for 30 minutes or until the potatoes are soft.

To Serve: Serve with plain boiled rice, or Red Lentil and Butter Rice (page 52), or Coconut Rice (page 53).

Makes 4 servings.

SPECIAL STEAMED HILSHA FISH

This is one of my favorite steamed fish dishes. It is a very popular dish in Burmese restaurants, known as *ngarthalauk baung*. Although the dish is called steamed, it is in fact cooked in a pot for almost a day.

The whole fish is full of tiny and medium bones. The fish is marinated with vinegar and lemon juice, then cooked for 6 to 8 hours until all the bones soften. It is a very appetizing dish because of the slightly sour taste due to the vinegar, lemon juice, and tomatoes. It has a strong aroma and tastes almost like tuna when cooked with tomatoes.

You can buy this frozen fish in some Indian food shops as the fresh ones are hard to find. The smallest fish I can find in the freezer is about 2 pounds. They need to be thawed for about half a day, then scaled and cleaned.

Use a nonstick saucepan to avoid burning the fish as the cooking time is exceptionally long for this dish.

Recipe and ingredients on next page

Ingredients

1 medium hilsha fish
(2 pounds)
3 tablespoons black vinegar
Juice of ½ small lemon
3 sticks lemongrass,
pounded well and cut
into 4 pieces each
1 large piece (1 inch) fresh
ginger, pounded
1 teaspoon turmeric powder
2½ tablespoons oil

6 cloves garlic, finely
chopped
1 teaspoon sweet paprika
3 fresh chilies, pounded
2 medium onions, cut into
thick rings
2 medium tomatoes, cut
into 8 pieces each
1 teaspoon salt
½ tablespoon fish sauce

Method

- Scale the fish and remove the insides. Cut into 3 pieces. Marinate fish with the vinegar and lemon juice for about ½ hour in a nonstick cooking pot.
- Add all the remaining ingredients and 3 cups water to the pot and bring to a boil. Cover and cook on very low heat. Check every hour to see if three is any water left in the pot. Add 1 cup water at a time and continue to cook. Repeat this process 5 to 6 times (hours) or until the bones almost melt in your mouth.

To Serve: Serve with plain boiled rice.

Makes 4 servings.

STEAMED FISH WITH ONIONS AND CHILIES

I would recommend using lime rather than lemon in this recipe as lime has a more distinctive taste and flavor especially when it is mixed with the light Chinese soy sauce. This dish must be served **immediately** at the peak of its flavor. The lime juice and chilies from the sauce make this simple steamed fish into a mouthwatering dish.

Tip: This dish is best made with freshly bought fish instead of frozen fish. Snapper fish tastes better than silver bream.

Ingredients
2 pounds snapper or silver bream fish (a whole fish and preferably fresh)
¼ teaspoon salt
1 small piece (¼ inch) fresh ginger, finely sliced
1 clove garlic, finely chopped
1 medium Spanish onion, finely sliced

Sauce
2 tablespoons Chinese light soy sauce
5 small fresh chilies, finely chopped
Juice of 1 big lime (or lemon)
¼ bunch Chinese parsley, finely chopped
3 cloves garlic, finely chopped

Method
- Scale fish. Wash and drain. Cut 2 slashes with knife on each side of the fish.
- Put fish on a plate. Rub fish with salt. Put some sliced ginger and chopped garlic inside the fish and inside the slashed portion of the fish.
- Steam the fish on a plate over medium to high heat for 20 to 25 minutes.

Continued

- Remove fish from the steamer and pour most of the water away, leaving only 2 tablespoons of fish stock.
- Sprinkle and cover fish with sliced onions. Add the remaining sauce ingredients in a bowl and mix well.
- Pour sauce mixture over steamed fish and serve hot.

To Serve: Serve with plain boiled rice.

Makes 4 servings.

SOUR DISHES:
A-CHIN-HIN

SOUR DISHES: A-CHIN-HIN

A-Chin means "sour" and Hin is "dish." More water is used for sour dishes than for *Sepyan* (curry). Sour sauce, combined with chilies, makes a hot and sour soup. The sour taste comes from vegetables such as turnips or the tamarind, which is used generously. Sour dishes are appetizing dishes. They accompany the curry or sepyan dishes very well to offset the rich taste.

ROSELLE LEAVES WITH SHRIMP

The vegetable used in this dish is called roselle and has a naturally sour taste. The bamboo shoots have a slightly sour taste as well but the shrimp and the fish paste balance the sour taste and add sweetness to the dish. These combine for a mouthwatering dish to eat with plain boiled rice. When cooked, the vegetables shrink and dissolve to create a slightly slimy appearance.

Although the roselle leaves are abundant and cheap in Myanmar it is quite the opposite in the Western countries. They are not easily obtainable and rather expensive. Look for them at Indian or Fijian markets.

Ingredients

5½ tablespoons oil	7 ounces roselle leaves, washed and drained
1 small onion, finely sliced	3 to 5 fresh chilies (for hotter taste)
3 cloves garlic, crushed	
½ teaspoon sweet paprika	3 ounces fresh bamboo shoots (optional)
¼ teaspoon turmeric powder	
3 ounces shrimps	1 teaspoon fish sauce

Method

- Add oil, onion, and garlic in a frying pan and fry over medium heat for about 3 minutes or until the onions are transparent. Add paprika and turmeric powder and mix.
- Add shrimps and fry for 2 minutes until they turn pink.
- Add roselle leaves and chilies, and fry well for about 5 minutes until all the vegetables shrink.
- Add bamboo shoots and fry for 2 to 3 minutes.
- Add fish sauce and fry for 2 to 3 minutes until all the ingredients are cooked thoroughly.

To Serve: This dish is served with either plain rice or Steamed Glutinous Rice with Nuts (page 183). The sour taste of the vegetables cooked with shrimp and fish paste is very appetizing.

Makes 4 servings.

PORK WITH BAMBOO SHOOTS

Fresh bamboo shoots from Asian groceries come in a clear plastic bag and are yellow in color. Canned bamboo shoots are not recommended. Pork adds a sweet taste to the bamboo shoots and chilies brings out their flavor. Bamboo shoots go well with pork and this is a delicious dish to try. Lean pork fillets are used in this recipe. However, for the best taste, use the three-layered pork (pork with a layer of skin, a layer of meat and a layer of fat) and cook until pork is very tender.

Ingredients

1½ pounds pork fillet
4 teaspoons fish sauce
2½ tablespoons oil
1 medium onion, finely
  sliced
3 cloves garlic, crushed
5 to 6 fresh chilies
1 small piece (¼ inch)
  fresh ginger, chopped or
  pounded
1 teaspoon sweet paprika
¼ teaspoon turmeric powder
8 ounces fresh bamboo
  shoots
1 teaspoon salt

Method

- Cut pork fillets into ½-inch pieces and marinate with fish sauce.
- Heat oil in frying pan. Add onion, garlic, ginger, and chilies and fry over medium heat until the onions are transparent.
- Add paprika and turmeric and fry for another minute.
- Add pork and fry for about 3 minutes or until the pork turns brown.
- Add bamboo shoots and fry for about 3 minutes.
- Add salt and 1½ cups water, cover and bring to a boil. Reduce heat and cook on low heat for about 30 minutes or until the pork and bamboo shoots are tender.

To Serve: Serve with plain boiled rice.

Makes 4 servings.

FISH WITH WHITE RADISH

The sour taste of this dish comes from three sources: radish, tomato, and tamarind juice. Red ocean perch is used as it cooks quickly and adds color to this dish. Note that only a small quantity of curry powder is added because this is not a curry dish and the emphasis is more on the sour taste. It is therefore optional to add the curry powder.

Ingredients

2 small onions, quartered
3 cloves garlic
1 small piece (¼ inch) fresh ginger
2½ tablespoons oil
1 small white radish, cut into thin rings
1 small soft tomato, sliced
3 to 4 fresh chilies
¼ teaspoon turmeric powder
1½ teaspoons sweet paprika
1 teaspoon curry powder
4 teaspoons fish sauce
½-inch cube tamarind, soaked in ¼ cup warm water
1 teaspoon salt
2 pounds ocean perch, scaled and cleaned
3 stems Chinese parsley

Method

- In a blender combine onion, garlic, and ginger and blend.
- Add oil and onion mixture in a saucepan and fry for about 3 minutes over medium heat until the onions are transparent.
- Add white radish, tomato, chilies, turmeric powder, paprika, and curry powder and fry for about 5 minutes.
- Add 2 cups water, fish sauce, tamarind juice, and salt and stir. Cover and boil for about 10 minutes or until the radishes are cooked.
- Add fish and cook for about 5 to 7 minutes on each side or until fish is cooked.
- Garnish with parsley.

To Serve: Serve with plain boiled rice.

Makes 4 servings.

FISH CAKE AND MIXED VEGETABLES WITH TAMARIND

A generous amount of tamarind used in this dish gives it a rather sour flavor and an appetizing taste. Sour dishes are usually included in the menu to offset other rich and spicy dishes.

Ready-made fish cakes can be bought easily in any Asian grocery store. Each fish cake package contains about 10 to 12 small, round fish cakes. For this dish, I usually cut each cake into 4 pieces. In Burma however, fish fillets (featherback) are bought and minced at home to prepare fresh homemade fish cakes.

Ingredients

1 medium turnip, skin removed	1 teaspoon curry powder
2 tablespoons oil	2 tablespoons fish sauce
1 medium onion, finely chopped	3 to 4 fresh long chilies, cut in half
4 cloves garlic, crushed	1 teaspoon salt
½ teaspoon turmeric powder	1 bunch watercress, cut in half
1 teaspoon sweet paprika	1 thick slice (1 inch) tamarind, soaked in ½ cup warm water and mixed well
1 package (7 ounces) fish cake, cut into 4 pieces	
1 small long eggplant, cut into wedges	15 okra
2 large tomatoes, cut into wedges	1 teaspoon fresh chili powder

Method

- Cut the turnip into 3 pieces. Take each piece and half it and slice into thin pieces.
- Heat oil in a saucepan. Fry onion, garlic, turmeric powder, and paprika over medium heat for about 3 minutes.
- Add fish cake, eggplant, turnip, tomatoes, turnip, and curry powder and fry over medium heat for 2 minutes.

- Add 2 cups water, fish sauce, chilies and salt. Bring to boil over high heat.
- Reduce to medium heat and cook for 15 minutes or until turnips and eggplants are soft.
- Add watercress and mix well until the vegetables dissolve and shrink in size.
- Reduce to low-medium heat. Add tamarind juice (including pieces) and boil for 3 minutes.
- Add okra and continue to boil for 5 minutes or until the okra are just cooked. Do not overcook as they may become slimy in appearance and taste.

To Serve: Scoop fish cake and vegetables onto a big bowl and sprinkle with fresh chili powder. Serve hot with plain boiled rice.

Makes 4 servings.

SALAD DISHES: A-THOKE

The following dishes are comparable to the Western salad dishes. The reason these dishes are classified as salads is because all the ingredients are added and tossed together to produce the final outcome. Traditionally, all the ingredients are placed on a plate and mixed by hands to blend the ingredients together. This technique of using the fingers to mix is called a-thoke. All the flavor from the ingredients, aroma of the fish sauce, and fragrance from lemon juice will make one salivate while preparing these dishes. Lime or lemon can be used in preparing these salads.

Salad dishes are more important to the Burmese than fried dishes, because the full flavor is captured from the fresh ingredients used. The tastes come from the chili (hot), tamarind or lemon (sour), shrimp paste (fishy), and fish sauce (salty). Often such tastes are combined in one dish to enjoy together.

I like to mention a few ingredients that enhance these salad dishes. If time permits, prepare them in advance and store them for later use. These ingredients are Fried Onions (page 109) Roasted Chickpea Powder (page 110) and Roasted Peanuts (page 111). Although optional, the fried onions add color, and flavor and add a sweet taste to any dish. I strongly recommend adding fried onions to salad dishes.

FRIED ONIONS

This is used as a garnish for most salad dishes. It adds a sweet taste and enhances the flavor of the dish. To me, a salad is not complete unless it has fried onions! Please note that this recipe produces "onion in oil." Some dishes may require the onion or the oil as separate ingredients. Other dishes may require both the onion and the oil to be used.

Ingredients
2 large onions
1 cup oil
1 teaspoon turmeric powder

Method
- Wash the onions. Slice finely and drain well until very dry.
- Add the oil, onions, and turmeric powder in a saucepan over medium heat and fry until the onions turn golden brown.
- Stir the onions occasionally to avoid burning. Switch off the heat immediately when the onions start to turn brown. Continue to cook in the hot oil.
- Remove the onions to a bowl and pour the oil into a separate bowl.

Makes 2 salad servings.

ROASTED CHICKPEA POWDER

Roasting or dry-frying means that the ingredient is placed in a frying pan and stirred slowly on low heat so that it will change color gradually without getting burned.

> **Ingredients**
> 1 cup chickpea powder

Method

- Preheat a nonstick fry pan without any fat. Once it is hot, reduce to low heat and add the chickpea powder.
- Cook slowly until brown, about 10 minutes. Note that one must be quite patient to roast the chickpea powder as it can take some time for the yellowish powder to turn brown. The heat must be low to avoid burning and the powder is stirred constantly allowing it to be roasted evenly.
- If a small amount is needed quickly, roast only 2 tablespoons to reduce cooking time.

ROASTED PEANUTS

If ready-made roasted and unsalted peanuts are available, then there is no need to roast the raw peanuts.

Ingredients
1 cup raw peanuts

Method

- Preheat a nonstick fry pan without any fat. Once it is hot, reduce to low heat and add the peanuts.
- Mix with a spatula to allow peanuts to be roasted evenly, about 5 minutes until brown.
- Remove peanuts and allow to cool down.
- Use a mortar and pestle to pound the peanuts. Alternatively, use the blender to blend them.

FISH CAKE SALAD

A type of fish called featherback is available in Burma and commonly used for this salad dish. Ready-made fish cakes packages can be bought in any Asian grocery store. They are convenient and easy to prepare.

Ingredients

½ tablespoon oil

1 package (7 ounces), ready-made fish cake

1 medium Spanish onion, washed and drained, and finely sliced

2 tablespoons fried onions (page 109)

½ small bunch Chinese parsley, finely chopped

2 tablespoons fish sauce

2 fresh chilies, finely chopped

Juice of 1 to 1½ lemons

Method

- Heat oil in a small frying pan. Add fish cake and fry lightly for about 1½ minutes on each side until golden brown.
- Remove fish cakes, let cool, thinly slice and transfer to a large plate.
- Add the remaining ingredients and mix together. Initially use only 1 lemon. Adjust taste by adding more lemon juice (sour) or fish sauce (salty).

To Serve: Serve with plain boiled rice, or Red Lentil and Butter Rice (page 52), or Coconut Rice (page 53).

Makes 4 servings.

LEMON AND ONION SALAD

This is a mouthwatering dish because the lemon flesh has a very refreshing taste. The sour taste of the lemons is balanced by the sweet shrimp powder and the fragrant grilled/roasted fish paste. In Burma, this is sometimes a recovery dish for people who suffered cold or flu and lost their appetite.

Ingredients
1 large lemon or 2 small ones
1 medium red onion
1 tablespoon sugar
2½ teaspoons fish paste
3 to 5 fresh chilies
2½ tablespoons dried shrimp, blended
¼ bunch Chinese parsley, finely chopped

Method
- Remove the skin from the lemon. Peel the flesh of the lemon and put on a plate.
- Slice onion very thinly. Rub with sugar and then wash and drain.
- Add fish paste and chilies in a nonstick frying pan. Fry for about 2 minutes on each side over low heat until fragrant and brown.
- Put roasted chilies and fish paste in a mortar and pound thoroughly with a pestle.
- Add fresh onions, pounded chilies mixture, shrimp powder, and parsley onto the lemon plate. Mix all the ingredients together.

To Serve: Serve with plain boiled rice, or Red Lentil and Butter Rice (page 52), or Coconut Rice (page 53). This is an excellent side dish to accompany curry dishes as well.

Makes 4 servings.

MANGO SALAD

Mango is a favorite fruit in Burma, eaten either hard and green or ripe. When green, it can be served in several ways and one way is to make salad. Mango salad can be eaten on its own or with boiled rice. Raw, firm, and sour mangoes are best to prepare this salad. The sourness of mango mixed with sweet fried onion, hot chilies, and salty fish paste make it very appetizing. It is one of my favorite dishes as it increases my appetite greatly. It serves as a nice snack on its own.

Many types of mangoes are available in Burma depending on the season, usually from April to June. Each type has a different shape, smell, and taste.

Ingredients
- 1 teaspoon fish paste
- 2 small raw and hard mangoes or 1 large mango, finely grated
- 1 small red onion, finely sliced
- 2½ tablespoons fried onions (page 109)
- 2½ tablespoons dried shrimp, blended
- ½ teaspoon fresh chili powder (optional)
- 1 tablespoon fried onion oil (page 109)

Method
- Grill fish paste for 2 minutes on each side. Pound it using a mortar and pestle when cooled.
- Add 1 cup grated mango, fresh onions, fried onions, grilled fish paste, dried shrimp, chili powder, and fried onion oil and mix them together.

To Serve: Serve with plain boiled rice, or Red Lentil and Butter Rice (page 52), or Coconut Rice (page 53).

Makes 4 servings.

PRAWN SALAD

To make this salad, the prawns can be either fried, grilled or boiled. If the prawns are boiled, the stock can be used to make Roselle Soup (page 163). This could be a sweet prawn salad dish if chilies are not added. This is another mouthwatering dish not to be missed. Fried prawns produce better salad taste.

Ingredients

½ pound king prawns
2 tablespoons oil
1 small Spanish onion (purple), finely sliced
½ cup finely sliced cucumber
2 stems Chinese parsley, finely chopped

1 teaspoon fish sauce
2 to 3 fresh chilies, finely chopped
Juice of ½ to 1 lemon
½ teaspoon fresh chili powder (optional)

Method

- Devein the prawns.

To fry the prawns: Remove shells. Add about 2 tablespoons oil in a saucepan. Quickly fry prawns over high heat for 3 to 4 minutes or until they turn pink.

To grill the prawns: Put under the grill and grill each side for 3 to 4 minutes until prawns turn pink. Let cool and remove shells.

To boil the prawns: Put prawns in a saucepan with just enough water (about 1 cup only) to cover the prawns and boil for 2 minutes or until the prawns turn pink. Let cool and remove shells.

Continued

- Cut prawns in half along length of body. Slice each half into thin pieces diagonally.
- Add sliced prawns, onions, cucumber, parsley, fish sauce, chilies, and lemon juice. Toss evenly. Add more fish sauce, lemon juice, or chili powder according to taste.

To Serve: Serve with plain boiled rice, or Red Lentil and Butter Rice (page 52), or Coconut Rice (page 53).

Makes 4 servings.

PENNYWORT SALAD

This plant can be grown in your backyard easily. Not much care is required except to water it occasionally. It is available year-round. We grow this and the small round green leaves give a nice and serene appearance. They look so beautiful and fresh after the rain.

To make salad pick a bunch of leaves from the garden, wash and remove half the stem leaving the leaves and part of the stem. The leaf has a slightly bitter taste when chewed and is followed by a cool sensation in your mouth that lingers for a short moment. Peanuts, dried shrimp, chickpea powder, and fried onions balance the bitter taste of the leaf.

Recent research has shown that pennywort may have properties that cure arthritis if fresh leaves are eaten daily. These leaves can be prepared in several ways. Eat these leaves with fish sauce mixed with some fresh chili powder. The leaves can also be used to prepare soups, or drinks. These leaves can be bought in Chinese, Vietnamese, or Western grocery stores.

Ingredients

1 bunch pennywort leaves (enough to produce about 1½ cups)
2 tiny red/purple onions, finely sliced
4 tablespoons fried onions (page 109)
1 to 2 teaspoons fish sauce
2½ tablespoons dried shrimp, blended
2 to 3 fresh chilies, finely chopped (optional)
1 tablespoon roasted chickpea powder (page 110)
2½ tablespoons crushed or pounded roasted peanuts (page 111)
Juice of 1 lemon
2 tablespoons fried onion oil
Fresh chili powder (optional)

Continued

Method

- Wash pennywort leaves and cut into thin strips (about 1½ cups).
- Add pennywort, fresh onions, 2 tablespoons fried onion, 1 teaspoon fish sauce, shrimp powder, chilies, chickpea powder, peanuts, half of lemon juice, and fried onion oil and toss or mix well until all the ingredients are well blended.
- Taste and add more fish sauce, lemon, or chili powder according to taste. Garnish salad with 1 more tablespoon fried onion.

To Serve: Serve with plain boiled rice, or Red Lentil and Butter Rice (page 52), or Coconut Rice (page 53).

Makes 4 servings.

GREEN TOMATO SALAD

In addition to your garden salad, try this dish with your barbeque and you will definitely enjoy this mouthwatering and delicious tomato salad. Hard green tomatoes are used in this recipe but you can also use semi-ripe tomatoes instead. Hard tomatoes will give a crisp taste.

Ingredients

2 medium firm green tomatoes, sliced into thin rings

1 small Spanish onion, finely sliced

2½ tablespoons fried onions (page 109)

2 teaspoons fish sauce

2½ tablespoons dried shrimp, blended

1 tablespoon roasted chick-pea powder (page 110)

2 fresh chilies, finely chopped (optional or more if hot taste is preferred)

1 stem Chinese parsley, finely chopped

1 shallot, finely chopped (optional)

1 teaspoon fried onion oil (page 110)

Juice of 1 lemon

Method

- Add all the ingredients, but use half of the lemon juice initially and mix evenly. Add more fish sauce, lemon juice, or chili powder according to taste.

To Serve: Serve with plain boiled rice, or Red Lentil and Butter Rice (page 52), or Coconut Rice (page 53).

Makes 4 servings.

GRILLED EGGPLANT SALAD

This is an unusual dish because the eggplant is grilled under hot charcoal which gives a very aromatic and woody fragrance.

Together with the peanuts and fried onions, it definitely is a sweet and creamy salad to be enjoyed.

A hot oven can be used instead of charcoal to create similar result. Note that after the eggplant is baked in the oven for about 45 minutes, it will produce a yellowish juice when the eggplant is sliced.

Ingredients
1 large round eggplant
1 tablespoon fried onions,
   (page 109)
1 teaspoon fried garlic
   (page 206)
1 tablespoon roasted and
   pounded peanuts
   (page 111)
¼ teaspoon salt

Method
- Preheat the oven to 470°F (250°C).
- Bake eggplant in oven. Turn the eggplant 2 to 3 times until all parts of the eggplant skin are evenly scorched and wrinkled. The eggplant should be steaming.
- Put the eggplant on a plate and remove or peel the scorched skin by holding the eggplant stem. Slice eggplant into pieces by holding the stem on a plate. Note the aromatic eggplant juice will pour out, but discard some of it.
- Add fried onion, fried garlic, pounded peanuts, and salt and mix lightly.

To Serve: Serve with plain boiled rice.

Makes 6 servings.

SIMPLE STIR-FRY DISHES: KYAW

SIMPLE STIR-FRY DISHES: KYAW

Anything that is fried is called *kyaw*. With stir-frying, it is important that all the vegetables are washed, drained, and dried well before they are fried. If the vegetables and meat are wet then instead of having the fried effect, they will be boiled and the vegetables will not be crispy.

Heat must be very high to capture and seal in the flavor. It is also important to have a big frying pan or big wok so that there is enough space to fry the vegetables evenly at the same time. The first few minutes are very important to cook the vegetable as this is the point when they capture the heat and give that fried aroma.

FRIED BITTER MELON WITH PRAWNS

The chilies enhance the bitter taste of the melon to create a bitter hot taste. If you want to try something different, I would recommend this dish. When I was young, I did not like bitter melon as it is very bitter. Now that I am older, my taste buds have changed to challenge different taste, including this dish.

Cook the bitter melon a bit longer until it is quite soft if you prefer. Otherwise, do not overcook it. If undercooked you will get a slightly raw but very crispy taste. Try both versions and discover your taste buds' desire. My mum usually cooks the first version whereas my father and I prefer the second version.

Ingredients

$\frac{1}{2}$ pound king prawns or 8 large king prawns, shells removed and deveined	1 small onion, finely sliced
	2 medium bitter melons, sliced into thin pieces
$\frac{1}{2}$ tablespoon fish sauce	2 to 3 chilies, pounded
2 tablespoons oil	$\frac{1}{2}$ teaspoon salt

Method
- Cut prawns into half-length and marinate with fish sauce.
- Heat oil in a wok and fry onion over medium heat for 2 minutes.
- Add prawns and stir-fry for about 2 minutes until they turn pink.
- Add bitter melon, and chilies and stir-fry for 1 to 2 minutes until the bitter melon blends well with other ingredients.
- Add salt and $\frac{1}{3}$ cup water and cook for 3 to 5 minutes until the melon becomes tender.

To Serve: Serve with plain boiled rice.

Makes 4 servings.

FRIED WATERCRESS WITH SHRIMP PASTE

In Burma, watercress is regarded as the poor people's dish as it is extremely cheap and upper class people do not usually eat this vegetable. Strangely, it is a popular dish in Asian restaurants in Australia and it is quite expensive to order.

To get the best results, wash and drain the watercress at least 2 hours before cooking. This will allow enough time for the vegetables to become dry and ready for frying. Garlic, chilies, and shrimp paste are an excellent combination that brings out the taste of watercress to give a hot, spicy, and delicious flavor. Shrimp paste usually comes in a block for slicing. If unavailable, fish paste may serve as a substitute.

Be warned that the ingredients will give off a strong aroma and so be ready to turn your exhaust fan on high to avoid the chili flavor getting into your throat!

Ingredients
1 bunch fresh watercress, washed and drained
1 slice (⅕ inch), shrimp or fish paste
2½ tablespoons oil
5 cloves garlic, finely sliced
3 to 4 fresh chilies, cut in half

Method
- Cut each watercress leaf or stalk in half or thirds.
- Dissolve shrimp or fish paste in 1 tablespoon warm water.
- Heat oil in a wok. Add garlic and chilies, and stir-fry over medium heat for 2 minutes.
- Increase to high heat. Add watercress and stir-fry quickly for 2 to 3 minutes until the vegetables dissolve and shrink.
- Add shrimp paste liquid and stir-fry quickly for 2 to 3 minutes.

To Serve: Serve with plain boiled rice.

Makes 4 servings.

FRIED EGGPLANTS WITH SHRIMP

The prawns and especially the shrimp paste bring out the flavor of the vegetables in this dish. The eggplant and the prawns add a sweet taste but the chilies add a contrasting hot taste. Personally, I think eggplant is tastier when a lot of chilies and shrimp paste are used. However, use less chili if you prefer a milder taste.

Ingredients

1 slice (¼ inch) shrimp paste	¼ pound fresh shrimps or 8 king prawns, shells removed and deveined
2 medium eggplants	2 fresh chilies, cut in half
2 ½ tablespoons oil	¼ teaspoon turmeric powder
2 cloves garlic, finely sliced	¼ teaspoon sweet paprika
1 small onion, finely sliced	

Method

- Dissolve shrimp paste in 1 tablespoon warm water.
- Wash and cut eggplants into fine slices.
- Heat oil in a wok, stir-fry garlic and onion over medium heat for 2 minutes.
- Add shrimps and stir-fry quickly until they turn pink.
- Add eggplants, chilies, turmeric powder, and paprika and stir-fry for about 2 minutes.
- Add dissolved shrimp paste solution and ¾ cup water and cook for 10 minutes or until eggplants are soft. Mix the eggplants occasionally to absorb the water. If the eggplants are still hard, add some more water (¼ cup) and continue to cook for 2 to 3 minutes.

To Serve: Serve with plain boiled rice.

Makes 4 servings.

This dish has a Chinese influence and Burmese people enjoy simple stir-fry dishes as an alternative to hot and spicy food. They offset the taste buds and are gentle on the stomach. A stir-fry is usually included as a separate dish for those who do not eat spicy meals.

One ingredient included in this dish has a strange name in Chinese that means "cloud ear fungus" when translated literally. It is sold dehydrated in packets. For cooking, soak in warm water for 15 minutes until it expands and softens.

Marinade
2 teaspoons Chinese light soy sauce
½ teaspoon Chinese dark soy sauce
1 teaspoon cornstarch

Ingredients
¼ pound pork fillet, thinly sliced
3½ tablespoons oil
1 medium onion, cut into 4 pieces
3 cloves garlic, pounded
½ small carrot, finely sliced
½ small capsicum, cut into slices
8 pieces Chinese cloud ear fungus
12 snow peas, cut in halves
1 cup cabbage, cut bite-size
2 stems spring onions, cut into ½-inch lengths
½ teaspoon salt

Method

- Soak cloud ear fungus in a bowl of warm water for 15 minutes. Wash with a little salt, drain, and finely slice.
- Mix pork with marinade ingredients for 15 minutes.
- Heat oil in a wok. Add onion, garlic and fry over high heat quickly for about 30 seconds.
- Add marinated pork and fry for about 2 minutes until almost cooked.
- Add carrot and capsicum and fry for 1 minute until almost cooked and soft.
- Add cloud ear fungus and fry for 1 minute.
- Add snow peas and fry for 1 minute.
- Add cabbage and fry for 1 minute.
- Add spring onion and salt and toss all the ingredients well for 1 minute.
- Add 1 tablespoon water and fry for 1 to 2 minutes.

To Serve: Serve with plain boiled rice.

Makes 4 servings.

FRIED BEEF SLICES WITH CURRY POWDER

Since this is a simple and quick stir-fry dish, the beef must be very tender to capture the flavor fully while cooking. Topside beef is highly recommended as it cooks quickly to seal the taste and flavor.

My father started this recipe and it was his idea to serve it with lemon wedges for a refreshing taste. My mum adds some tomatoes and parsley to enhance the color and flavor. Then I suggested some mint to add extra fragrance.

Marinade

2 teaspoons fish sauce
½ teaspoon cornstarch
¼ teaspoon turmeric powder
½ teaspoon sweet paprika
2 teaspoons curry powder

Ingredients

1 pound tender topside beef
4 tablespoons oil
1 medium onion, finely sliced
1 tomato, thinly sliced
¼ cup chopped Chinese parsley, cut into ½-inch pieces
10 mint leaves, finely chopped
Lemon wedges

Method

- Combine all marinade ingredients. Cut beef into thin fillets and marinate for about 15 minutes.
- Heat oil in a wok. Add onion and fry for 1 minute over medium to high heat.
- Add tomato and fry for 2 minutes over high heat.
- Add marinated beef and stir-fry quickly for 2 minutes over high heat.
- Add 1½ tablespoons water, parsley, and mint and stir-fry well for another minute.

To Serve: Put beef on a plate and garnish with lemon wedges. Squeeze lemon over beef before serving.

Makes 4 servings.

FRIED CHICKEN WITH CHILIES

This dish is quite dark because of the dark soy sauce. The chilies are fried until dark in color and the oil is then reused to cook the chicken. If you want to try something different with chicken this is a delicious dish. Generous quantities of chilies are used to create a hot taste dish but the sweet soy sauces balance them well.

Initially, I cut my chicken into ½-inch pieces until I saw in Burma that the chicken pieces are very small. So I changed my recipe to smaller pieces so they can cook quickly and seal in the flavor.

Ingredients

1 chicken breast
1 small piece (¼ inch) fresh ginger, blended or pounded to make juice
¼ teaspoon salt
2½ tablespoons oil
8 to 12 long red chilies, washed and dried
1 medium onion, diced into small cubes
3 cloves garlic, finely chopped
1 tablespoon Chinese light soy sauce
4 teaspoons Chinese dark soy sauce
¼ cup cashew nuts (optional)

Method

- Cut chicken fillets into ¼-inch cubes and marinate with ginger and salt.
- Heat oil on low heat in a wok. Add chilies and fry for 1 to 2 minutes on each side or until they are brown/black and crispy. Remove the chilies from the wok.
- Increase to high heat and add onion, and garlic and fry for about 2 minutes until the onions are soft.

- Add chicken pieces and fry over high heat for 3 to 5 minutes or until the chicken pieces are quite cooked.
- Add in fried chilies and light and dark soy sauces and fry for 3 to 5 minutes.
- Top chicken dish with cashew nuts.

To Serve: Serve with plain boiled rice.

Makes 4 servings.

FRIED CHILI PRAWNS

It is recommended to blend the onion, garlic, ginger and chili together or pound them well to bring out the full flavor and produce a delicious hot dish.

Ingredients
1 pound king prawns or
   medium-size prawns
1 teaspoon fish sauce
½ teaspoon salt
½ teaspoon sweet paprika

3 cloves garlic
1 medium onion, quartered
3 to 4 small chilies or
   1 long chili
5½ tablespoons oil

Method

- Remove the prawn head and shells, devein and marinate with fish sauce, salt, and paprika.
- In a blender, combine garlic, onion and chilies and blend well.
- Heat oil in a wok. Add onion mixture and sauté over medium heat for 8 to 10 minutes or until onions are transparent.
- Add prawns and stir-fry for about 4 minutes until prawns curl into a circular shape and turn pink. Add 1½ tablespoons water and fry for 1 more minute.

To Serve: Serve with plain boiled rice.

Makes 4 servings.

FRIED GOURD WITH SHRIMP

Shrimp and gourd go very well together to produce a sweet flavor but the chilies add a contrasting hot taste. This dish can be enjoyed as a meal or hot and sweet soup.

Calabash Gourd, a type of melon, adds extra sweetness to the chicken and the soup. This is a very popular melon in Burma, as it can be cooked in several different ways. It can be fried in batter, cooked with meat or prawns, or simply made into soup.

Ingredients

1 small gourd (about 2 pounds)
2½ tablespoons oil
1 medium onion, finely sliced
4 cloves garlic, pounded
1 small piece (¼ inch) fresh ginger, thinly sliced
½ pound shrimps, heads removed
1 thin slice (¼ inch) fish paste
¼ teaspoon sweet paprika
Salt (optional)

Method

- Peel skin from the gourd and divide into ½-inch lengths. Cut each piece into ¼-inch chunks.
- Soak in water to avoid browning, drain well before cooking.
- Dissolve shrimp paste in 1 tablespoon warm water.
- Heat oil in a small pot. Add onion, garlic, and ginger and fry over high heat for about 3 minutes.
- Add shrimp and fry for about 2 minutes until the shrimps turn pink.
- Add gourd pieces and fry about 2 minutes.
- Add shrimp paste solution and paprika, and fry for about 1 minute.
- Add 1 cup water, cover and bring to a boil over high heat. Reduce to medium heat and continue to cook for 10 to 13 minutes or until the gourds are soft. Add salt to taste.

To Serve: Serve with plain boiled rice.
Makes 4 servings.

FIRM TOFU WITH BEAN SPROUTS

This is a simple vegetarian dish. In a typical Burmese market, you may find both fresh tofu and bean sprouts together, as these are the main ingredients for this and many other dishes. The buyers are free to select the number of tofu slices and the amount of bean sprouts they want to buy. In Western countries, however, everything is available in a neat plastic bag. There are several types of tofu and so select the firm tofu (either in white or yellow) as opposed to soft tofu. The tofu is fried first and then the bean sprouts are added and stir-fried quickly to maintain its crispness and crunchiness. Whether you are a vegetarian or non-vegetarian, you will love this.

The Burmese mix Monosodium Glutamate (MSG) and sugar in equal proportion to reduce their intake of MSG. This combination, along with turmeric, improves tofu's blandness and gives a nice color.

Please be cautious when using MSG, as it may cause a severe allergic reaction in some people.

Ingredients

1 package (16 ounces) firm tofu

1 teaspoon monosodium glutamate (MSG, optional)

1 tablespoon sugar (optional)

½ teaspoon turmeric (optional)

3 tablespoons oil

1 medium onion, sliced finely

4 to 5 fresh chilies

1 package bean sprouts (15 ounces), washed and drained

½ tablespoon Chinese light soy sauce

1 teaspoon salt

3 stems shallot, cut into ½ inch lengths

Method

- Cut tofu into $1/4$-inch-wide slices. Rub each piece with MSG and sugar mixture and turmeric.
- Heat oil in a wok. Add tofu slices and fry over medium to high heat for 2 to 3 minutes on each side until golden brown. Remove tofu and drain.
- Increase to high heat; add onion and chilies and fry for 1 minute.
- Add bean sprouts and salt and stir-fry quickly for 1 minute.
- Return tofu to the wok. Add soy sauce and shallots and stir for 1 more minute.
- Add $1\frac{1}{2}$ tablespoons water (if too dry) and fry for half a minute only. Do not fry for too long as the bean sprouts will be over-cooked and lose their crispiness.

To Serve: Serve with plain boiled rice or on its own.

Makes 4 servings.

DIPS OR SIDE DISHES: DOOKE-SAYAR

DIPS OR SIDE DISHES: DOOKE-SAYAR

Dooke-sayar refers to any side dishes that accompany the main course. Burmese people love side dishes as they complement the taste of the main meal. They can be a hot gravy sauce or simply just a paste that has been grilled and pounded using chili and garlic. Raw or boiled vegetables are dipped into the sauce or paste.

For low-budget people in Burma, a side dish could be treated as main dish if is served with rice. A slice of grilled shrimp or fish paste could be used as a dip to accompany boiled gourd fruits or leaves.

CHILI TOMATO SAUCE

Usually, this side dish is accompanied by various raw or boiled vegetables, which are dipped into the sauce and then eaten with rice. Common vegetables are lettuce, cucumber, red radishes, Chinese parsley, and cabbage.

This is a very nice dish to enjoy especially during summer. Cold and crispy lettuce leaves topped with this hot tomato gravy can be served as an entrée or with rice.

Ingredients
2½ tablespoons oil
1 medium onion, finely chopped
3 cloves garlic, finely chopped
2½ tablespoons dried shrimp, soaked in warm water, drained and finely chopped
3 medium ripe tomatoes, sliced
3 to 5 chilies, sliced into 3 pieces each
½ teaspoon turmeric powder
1 teaspoon sweet paprika
½ tablespoon fish sauce
1 slice (¼ inch) shrimp paste
½ teaspoon salt
Chinese parsley for garnish

Method
- Dissolve shrimp paste in 1 tablespoon warm water.
- Add oil, onion, and garlic in frying pan or wok and fry over medium heat for about 5 minutes.
- Add shrimp and stir quickly.
- Add tomatoes, chilies, turmeric powder, and chili powder and stir-fry for 4 to 5 minutes or until tomatoes are dissolved.
- Add fish sauce, shrimp paste solution, salt, and 2 tablespoons water and simmer on low heat for 3 to 5 minutes.
- Garnish with some fresh parsley.

To Serve: This tomato dish is served with fresh parsley, lettuce, cucumber, or small radishes. Serve with boiled rice if desired.
Makes 4 servings.

This dish is very simple and easy to prepare. The sweet and sour and hot taste complements any fried noodles or offsets an oily dish.

Ingredients

1 large cucumber or 3 small Lebanese cucumbers

4 to 5 fresh chilies, sliced diagonally into 3 pieces each

2 teaspoons white vinegar

1½ teaspoons white sugar

Method

- Remove the skin from the cucumber and remove the core by cutting in half. Further slice the halved cucumber into thin slices again.
- Place all the ingredients in a bowl, mix together, and serve chilled.

To Serve: This is a good side dish for Special Steamed Hilsha Fish (page 91) to offset its richness.

Makes 4 servings.

SWEET AND SOUR TOMATO AND CABBAGE PICKLES

This is an easily prepared side dish to serve with the main course.

Ingredients

1 medium tomato, thinly sliced
1 small Spanish onion, thinly sliced
1 cup finely sliced cabbage
1 tablespoon chopped spring onions
1 teaspoon white vinegar
4 teaspoons white sugar
¼ teaspoon salt

Method

- Place all the ingredients in a bowl, mix together and serve.

To Serve: This is especially a good accompaniment to any fried noodles.

Makes 4 servings.

FRIED SHRIMP WITH SHRIMP PASTE

This dish is called *balachung* in Burmese. Burmese people usually cook balachung, then store it in an airtight container and serve it whenever they desire. It is convenient to serve when an extra dish is on call. Those who like it hot could add 1 to 2 teaspoons of hot chili powder.

Balachung could almost be treated as an entrée or a snack! Cucumber is the most popular vegetable to accompany it but the choice is yours to be discovered.

One thing I miss eating with the *balachung* is a type of pod called *danyia*. It is a fruit-like pod, which has to be boiled and the skin removed before eating. It has a bitter taste and some pods are crunchy while other pods are chewy.

Ingredients

¼ cup sliced shrimp paste
1 package (6 ounces) dried shrimp
1 ounce dried tamarind
¾ cup oil
½ teaspoon turmeric powder
2 medium onions, thinly sliced
1 whole garlic, sliced into rings
½ teaspoon sugar
½ teaspoon salt
2 teaspoons sweet paprika
5 fresh chilies

Method

- Dissolve shrimp paste in 2 tablespoons warm water and mash well.
- Soak shrimp in warm water for about 10 minutes and drain well. Blend shrimp in a blender.
- Soak tamarind in ½ cup warm water for about 15 minutes and squeeze to extract the juice.

- Heat oil and turmeric powder in a frying pan. Add onions and fry over medium heat for 10 to 15 minutes or until golden brown and crispy. Remove onions from the oil and drain them.
- Add garlic rings to the frying pan and fry over low-medium heat until golden brown and crispy. Remove garlic and drain well.
- Remove most of the oil leaving only about 1 tablespoon in the frying pan.
- Reduce to low heat and add shrimp paste solution, sugar, salt, and paprika.
- Add blended shrimp and tamarind juice and stir-fry for about half a minute.
- Return the fried onions, and fried garlic, chilies and combine all the ingredients for about 2 minutes on low heat.

To Serve: Traditionally, sliced cucumber will be served with the balachung. Alternately, boiled cabbage leaves or small raw radishes are also served.

Makes 6 servings.

DRIED SHRIMP AND FISH SAUCE

This is a simple dish to prepare, as all the ingredients are usually available at home. This sauce is commonly used to dip fresh pennywort leaves, small red radishes, or green mangoes. It is quite a hot and salty dish, served to offset or balance spicy or rich curry dishes and to add some taste to the raw vegetables. Note that this dish is served in very small amounts.

Ingredients
4 teaspoons oil
½ cup dried shrimp, pounded or blended
4 teaspoons fish sauce
1 teaspoon vinegar (white or brown)
1 teaspoon fresh chili powder

Method
- Heat oil in a frying pan on low heat.
- Add blended shrimp and mix quickly.
- Add fish sauce and vinegar and blend briefly.
- Add fresh chili powder and mix well.

To Serve: This is also a great accompaniment to the Special Steamed Hilsha Fish (page 91) or any of the curry dishes.

Makes 6 servings.

POUNDED GRILLED SHRIMP PASTE AND GARLIC

This paste is eaten in small amounts only to add extra pungent and tangy flavor to curry dishes. Small red radishes are excellent accompaniments to this paste.

Ingredients

1 tablespoon shrimp paste
4 teaspoons dried shrimp, pounded or blended
5 cloves garlic
2 fresh chilies
1 fresh lime, cut into wedges

Method

- Dry-fry the shrimp paste, garlic, and chilies in a small nonstick pan for about 5 minutes over low heat. Turn each side after a few minutes until all are dried, crispy, brown, and fragrant.
- Alternatively, place them under a broiler and grill for about 2 minutes on each side.
- Put all the grilled ingredients and shrimp in a mortar and pound into a paste using a pestle.
- Before serving, squeeze lime over the paste if desired.

To Serve: This is a great accompaniment to any of the curry dishes. It can be served with red radishes or used as a chutney.

Makes 6 servings.

INSTANT FISH SAUCE DIP

This is a very easy dip that is prepared almost instantaneously. Fresh or raw vegetables can be dipped into this salty sauce. It is a mouthwatering dip to munch and crunch sour green mangoes and is sure to make your mouth water.

Ingredients
1½ tablespoons fish sauce
¼ teaspoon dried chili
   powder

Method
- Put the ingredients in a small bowl and mix well.

To Serve: Serve fish sauce dip with cucumber slices, pennywort leaves, and green mango slices.

Makes 1½ tablespoons.

SOUP: HIN-YAWE

In Burma, soup (known as *hin-yawe*) is served as part of, but not before, the main meal. This is because soup is used to quench the thirst between courses instead of soft drinks found in many Western homes.

There are basically two types of soups: sweet and bitter or peppery soup. *Hin-cho* is clear sweet soup with only some vegetables added, without too much garlic or pepper. *Hin-ngar* is a bit more elaborate in the sense that there are a lot of ingredients and generous amounts of garlic and hot peppers added to the soup.

Basically, the soup stock is made from chicken, pork, fish, fresh shrimp or more commonly from dried shrimp. They are boiled for some time and the desired vegetables are added in just before serving along with a sprinkle of some pepper. Fish can be grilled to enhance the flavor of the fish stock.

Unlike the Chinese soups, which are cooked in big pots, the Burmese soups are cooked in small quantities. The quickest soup involves boiling one bowl of water with some dried shrimp for a few minutes and add some gourd leaves or bean sprouts and topping with some pepper.

There are many types of soups that can be made. Unfortunately, most vegetables required are not found in the West. I have included those recipes where the ingredients are readily available. Other commonly used vegetables for soup are concinna leaves, which are small leaves with prickled branches; pennywort leaves; gourd leaves; bean sprouts; and cabbage leaves.

Usually a bowl of soup is placed in the center of the table from which people help themselves. Nowadays, hygiene-conscious people have their own individual bowl of soup. Soup is served piping hot regardless of the hot weather.

PEPPER AND GARLIC FISH SOUP WITH VERMICELLI

This is one of the popular soups that accompany the Hand-Mixed Noodle Salad (page 202). This soup is always served piping hot to bring out the garlic and pepper flavor.

This is an excellent soup for wintertime as pepper and a generous amount of garlic are used to combat cold weather and the flu. The glass vermicelli, Chinese cloud ear fungus (see page 128 for details), and dried banana leaves can be purchased from most Chinese shops.

The real taste of this soup comes from the amount of pepper one dares to try. If your nose is not running you have not really experienced it yet.

Ingredients

25 pieces Chinese cloud ear fungus

1 small flathead fish (0.7 pound), scaled, washed, and drained

2½ tablespoons fish sauce

10 to 12 cloves garlic, pounded

1 medium piece (½ inch) fresh ginger, cut into pieces

25 strands dried banana leaves, soaked in warm water, drained and finely sliced

½ small package glass vermicelli (1½ ounces), soaked in water and cut in half

½ teaspoon salt

2 teaspoons crushed black pepper

Method

- Soak cloud ear fungus in a bowl of warm water for 15 minutes. Wash with a little salt, drain and finely slice.
- Add 6 cups water, fish, fish sauce, garlic, and ginger in a pot and bring to a boil. Reduce and simmer for 20 minutes. Remove fish from the saucepan and let it cool.

Continued

- Add cloud ear fungus, banana leaves, vermicelli, salt, and pepper and boil on low heat for about 15 minutes.
- Remove bones from the fish to extract the fish fillets. Return fish fillets back to the soup pot and continue to boil for 15 minutes on low heat.

To Serve: Serve with the Hand-Mixed Noodle Salad (page 202). Top with more pepper for hotter taste in individual bowl.

Makes 4 servings.

SIMPLE SHRIMP AND VERMICELLI SOUP

This is an economical soup to prepare for those people in Burma with low budgets. It could almost pass as vegetarian soup since only a small amount of shrimp is used.

Ingredients

10 pieces Chinese cloud ear
  fungus (see page 128)
10 strips dried banana
  leaves
4 cloves garlic
25 to 30 fresh shrimps,
  shells removed

2 teaspoons oil
1 package (1.76 ounces)
  vermicelli, soaked in
  water for about ½ hour
1 tablespoon fish sauce
¼ to ½ teaspoon salt
1 teaspoon whole black
  peppercorns

Method

- Soak cloud ear fungus in a bowl of warm water for 15 minutes. Wash with a little salt, drain and finely slice.
- Soak dried banana leaves in a bowl of warm water for 10 minutes. Wash, drain, and cut into pieces.
- Pound garlic first and then pound the shrimp lightly.
- Heat oil in a small pot. Add garlic and shrimp mixture and fry over medium heat for 1 to 2 minutes.
- Add in 3½ cups water and bring to a boil. Add vermicelli, fungus, dried banana leaves, fish sauce, and salt and boil for 7 minutes.
- In a small frying pan, pan-fry the peppercorns for about 2 minutes over low heat.
- Add lightly crushed peppercorns to the soup and boil for 3 minutes. Add more fish sauce if required.

To Serve: Serve hot, on its own or with Hand-Mixed Noodle Salad (page 202).

Makes 2 to 4 small servings.

SPLIT PEA AND PRAWN SOUP

This is my favorite soup. The beautiful fragrance from the fried prawns and the bay leaves enhance the spilt pea flavor. The onion adds extra sweetness and the boiled peas create a creamy soup.

Ingredients

1½ cups split peas
1 tablespoon oil
1 medium onion, finely chopped
10 king prawns, heads removed and deveined
1 small piece (¼ inch) fresh ginger, cut into pieces
3 bay leaves
1 teaspoon salt

Method

- Soak split peas in cold water for about an hour. Wash and drain.
- Heat oil in a pot and add onion and fry over medium heat for about 2 minutes.
- Add prawns and fry for about 2 minutes until prawns turn pink.
- Add drained split peas and fry for 1 minute.
- Add 6 cups water and ginger and bring to a boil on high heat. Do not cover as it may boil over. When it is boiling, scoop the bubbles from the surface.
- Add bay leaves and salt and reduce to medium heat and continue to boil for about 30 minutes or until the peas are tender.

To Serve: Serve with any main meal or on its own.

Makes 4 servings.

CHICKEN AND TOMATO SOUP

This simple sweet soup is topped with pepper and parsley to enhance the taste. It is not thick or creamy but rather watery. Bones of a whole chicken can be used to make the chicken stock. Alternatively, if canned chicken broth is used, add two (14-ounce) cans of chicken broth instead of water and reduce the simmering time to only 20 minutes.

Ingredients

2 teaspoons oil
1 medium onion
5 chicken breast bones, washed and drained
1 can (15 ounces) tomatoes or 3 medium ripe tomatoes, cut into 8 pieces
4 teaspoons fish sauce
1 teaspoon salt
1 small piece (¼ inch) fresh ginger, cut into pieces
2 stems spring onions, finely chopped
¼ bunch Chinese parsley, finely chopped
¼ teaspoon pepper

Method

- Heat oil in a saucepan. Add onion and chicken bones and fry for about 5 minutes on medium heat.
- Add tomatoes and fry until tomatoes are soft.
- Add 4½ cups water, fish sauce, salt, and ginger. Cover and bring to boil on medium heat for about 5 minutes. Reduce heat and simmer for about 45 minutes.

To Serve: Serve soup in a small bowl and top with spring onion and parsley for flavor. Sprinkle with pepper for hotter taste and serve hot. This soup is best accompanied by Mandalay Chicken Noodle (page 207).

Makes 4 servings.

HOT AND SOUR SOUP

This dish was adopted from Thailand, Burma's neighboring country. The flavor of this soup comes from the lemongrass and lemon juice. Three pieces of chicken bones are used to make the chicken stock. Alternatively, remove the fillets of a chicken and use the bones to make stock. Cans of quail eggs (with or without shells) are available from most Asian grocery stores.

Ingredients

½ cup finely sliced chicken breast fillets
4 teaspoons fish sauce
3 chicken breast bones, washed and drained
1 small piece (¼ inch) fresh ginger, pounded
2 teaspoons oil
2 stalks lemongrass, cut into 4 pieces each and pounded
2 fresh long chilies, cut into 4 pieces each
2 medium tomatoes, cut into 8 pieces each
8 fish balls, cut into halves
8 to 12 quail eggs
½ cup straw mushrooms
Juice of ¼ to ½ lemon
¼ teaspoon sugar
¼ to ½ teaspoon salt
8 medium king prawns, shells removed and deveined
½ cup finely chopped Chinese parsley, chopped finely

Method

- Mix sliced chicken with fish sauce for 15 minutes.
- Add chicken bones, ginger and 7 cups water in a saucepan and boil over medium heat for about 40 minutes to make chicken stock.
- Heat oil in a separate saucepan. Add lemongrass and chilies and fry over medium heat for about 2 minutes.
- Add tomatoes and fry for about 4 minutes or until tomatoes are thoroughly cooked.

- Add sliced chicken pieces, and fish balls and fry about 4 minutes.
- Add 4 cups of chicken stock and bring to boil over medium heat.
- Add quail eggs, straw mushrooms, lemon juice, sugar, and salt and simmer over low heat for about 25 minutes.
- Just before serving, increase to medium heat, add prawns and boil for 5 minutes. Top soup with chopped parsley.

To Serve: Serve hot with any main meal or as an entrée.

Makes 4 servings.

PENNYWORT SOUP

This is regarded as cooling soup because the leaves supposedly cool the internal organ of body such as the liver (or reduce heat from too much fried food).

Pennywort can be grown year-round. It is available from Thai, Vietnamese, Chinese, or even Western grocery stores.

Ingredients
2 pounds pork bones
1 medium piece (½ inch)
  fresh ginger, cut into
  pieces

2 bunches pennywort,
  washed and drained
1 teaspoon salt

Method
- Add 4 cups water in a saucepan and bring to a boil on medium heat. When boiling, add pork bones and boil for 3 minutes or until the blood is drained. Pour the water away and rinse the pork bones.
- Add 8 cups water and ginger and boil for about 15 minutes on high heat.
- Add pennywort leaves and boil for 10 minutes. Reduce to low heat and simmer for 45 to 60 minutes. Add salt to taste.

To Serve: Serve with any main meal, but avoid hot dishes for that day.

Makes 4 servings.

ROSELLE SOUP

Roselle leaves are naturally sour and adding several hot chilies will make this into a hot and sour soup. Fish paste complements the sour leaves well. Hot and sour soups are very good to promote appetite and balance rich and creamy meals. Try Indian or Fijian shops for the roselle leaves.

Ingredients
2 teaspoon oil
1 small onion
2 to 3 fresh chilies
½ pound small shrimps, deveined leaving the shells
1 small piece (¼ inch) fresh ginger, sliced

1 teaspoon shrimp paste, dissolved in 1 tablespoon warm water
6 ounces roselle leaves, washed and drained
½ teaspoon salt

Method
- Add oil, onion, and chilies in a pot and fry over medium heat for about 2 minutes.
- Add shrimp and fry for about 2 minutes.
- Add 2½ cups water, ginger, and shrimp paste solution and bring to a boil.
- Add roselle leaves and bring to a boil again. Reduce to low heat and simmer for 20 minutes to bring out the sourness of the leaves. Add salt to taste.

To Serve: Serve with any main meal, especially to offset rich curry dishes.

Makes 4 servings.

PORK SPARERIBS WITH FERMENTED MUSTARD SOUP

This very popular soup in Burma can be prepared using either pork or duck meat. I have used pork, as the spareribs are easier to buy and prepare.

If using duck meat, remove the skin completely. Cut half a bird into small pieces, add plenty of ginger and allow for a longer cooking time.

Fermented mustard comes in a plastic bag and has a yellow color. It can be purchased in most Chinese grocery stores.

Ingredients
1 strip pork spareribs (1 pound)
1 teaspoon salt
1 tablespoon fish sauce
4 cloves garlic, pounded well
¼ teaspoon turmeric
1 small piece (¼ inch) fresh ginger, cut into small pieces
1 bag (12 ounces) fermented mustard, washed, drained and thinly sliced

Method
- Cut sparerib strip into ½-inch pieces and marinate with the salt, fish sauce, garlic, and turmeric for 15 minutes.
- Put marinated spareribs in a soup pot; add 4 cups water, and the ginger and bring to a boil over high heat.
- Reduce to low heat, add mustard leaves and simmer for about 30 minutes. Stir the soup occasionally. Serve hot.

To Serve: Serve with any main meal.

Makes 4 servings.

ASSORTED FRITTERS: A-KYAW

ASSORTED FRITTERS: A-KYAW

Fritters are enjoyed throughout the day, especially in the morning as a breakfast treat. They can be eaten on their own or as an accompaniment to those soup noodles mentioned in the Special Occasion section of this book (page 193-208). They are especially nice during winter mornings when they are served with piping hot Burmese tea.

The fritters are made from various presoaked peas and sliced vegetables. They are then dipped into batter and fried in deep oil. This is similar to the Japanese tempura except that the batter is slightly thicker. Fritters are enjoyed straight from the frying pan so that they are hot and crispy.

Fritters are served with various types of sauces and lettuce leaves. They usually accompany Burmese tea as it quenches the thirst and washes down the oiliness of the fritters. In Western countries, people usually go for soft drinks or beer.

Fritter sellers are mostly situated in a corner shop under a thatched hut or in the markets. One of the most popular places is near the university campus where students meet friends for light snacks.

ASSORTED VEGETABLE FRITTERS

The most common vegetables used in Burma are gourd, onion, watercress, and potato. Split pea and chickpea are also very popular.

One ladyfinger banana is added to the batter, which strangely enough adds a reddish tint to the fried fritters.

Ingredients	Batter
1 small gourd	1 cup rice flour
1 medium potato	½ cup glutinous rice flour
1 small choko	½ teaspoon turmeric powder
2 onions, sliced into rings	1 teaspoon salt
Oil for frying	1 small ladyfinger banana, mashed

Method

- Cut the gourd, potato, and choko into 1-inch pieces.
- Mix all the batter ingredients in a bowl.
- Add 1 cup water in gradually and stir well to form a smooth batter. Ensure that the batter is quite thick and not too watery.
- Heat oil in a deep frying pan. Reduce to medium heat before frying.
- Dip a few pieces of gourd, potato, choko, or onion into the batter and then put into the frying pan. Turn fritters frequently and fry until golden brown. Remove and drain on paper towels.
- Continue to fry until the mixture is finished.

To Serve: Usually these fritters are served with lettuce leaves and Special Tamarind, Chili, and Garlic Sauce (page 205).

Makes 4 servings.

FRIED SPLIT PEAS

This is a favorite snack, usually eaten with Rice Noodles with Fish Gravy (page 198). It adds crunchiness and enhances the taste of the soup. I always insist that my mum prepare this snack to serve with this noodle soup. Otherwise, I find that this noodle soup is not complete and something is missing.

You need to soak the split peas overnight, otherwise the peas will be very hard to bite. A quicker method is to add 1 teaspoon of baking powder and soak for 3 hours prior to cooking.

Note that this is an extremely watery batter.

Ingredients	Batter
³/₄ cup dried yellow split peas	1 cup rice flour
	1 teaspoon turmeric powder
5 cups oil for frying	½ cup glutinous rice flour
	3 cups water
	1 teaspoon salt

Method
- Soak the peas overnight and drain ½ hour before cooking
- Mix all the batter ingredients in a bowl to make a watery batter.
- Add strained peas to the batter.
- Heat oil in a frying pan.
- Scoop the pea mixture (about ¼ cup) in a saucer and pour the mixture into the pan and fry. Turn each side and fry until golden brown. Remove and drain on paper towels.
- Continue to fry until the mixture is finished.
- Let cool. Crush into small pieces and put in an airtight container.

To Serve: Best to serve with Rice Noodles with Fish Gravy (page 198) or enjoy them as a snack.

Makes 6 to 8 servings.

SHRIMP WITH BEAN SPROUT FRITTERS

This is a mouthwatering snack to be enjoyed on its own or served with chilie sauce. The shrimp fried in batter produce a delicious fragrance. Such snacks are available in the market stalls and along the roadsides in Yangon.

The following ingredients produce seven fritters, each about the size of a burger. Make sure that the bean sprouts are well drained to avoid oil splashing when fried.

Batter
½ cup rice flour
¼ cup glutinous rice flour
½ teaspoon turmeric powder
¾ teaspoon salt

Ingredients
4 to 5 cups oil, for frying
½ pound shrimp, heads and tails removed, washed and drained
2 cups bean sprouts

Method
- Combine the batter ingredients with ½ cup water in a bowl to make a smooth batter.
- Heat oil in a deep frying pan over medium heat.
- To make each shrimp cake, scoop ¾ tablespoon batter, about 10 shrimps and a handful of bean sprouts and put on a small saucer. Mix the ingredients quickly and spread the mixture evenly out on a saucer.

Continued

- Pour the shrimp mixture from the saucer into the hot oil slowly and fry over medium heat for about 1½ minutes on each side until golden brown. Remove and drain on paper towels.
- Continue to fry until the ingredients are finished.

To Serve: This dish is best served with the Special Tamarind, Chili, and Garlic Sauce (page 205) and Burmese tea to wash down the oiliness and to quench the thirst.

Makes 4 servings.

FRIED YELLOW SPLIT PEA CAKE

This is a popular snack sold in the markets or on the roadsides. It is an Indian dish and therefore, usually made and sold by Indian people. The following mixture makes about 10 split pea cakes. It is an excellent dish to serve as an entrée or as a snack. Add a few chilies for hotter taste and mint for fragrance.

Ingredients

½ cup dried yellow split peas
1 teaspoon baking powder
15 mint leaves, finely chopped
1 small onion, finely sliced
3 small fresh chilies
½ teaspoon turmeric powder
½ teaspoon sweet paprika
1 teaspoon salt
Oil for frying

Method

- Wash peas and soak in warm water with baking powder for about 3 hours. Drain well before cooking.
- Using a blender or mortar and pestle, blend or pound the split peas until well mashed. Note: do not add water to blend!
- Add the mint, onion, chilies, turmeric, paprika, and salt and continue to blend or pound for 1 minute.
- Heat oil in a frying pan.
- Take ½ to 1 tablespoon of the pea mixture and roll it into a ball. Dip it into the hot oil and fry over medium heat on each side until golden brown. Remove and drain on paper towels.
- Continue to fry until the mixture is finished.

To Serve: Serve as a snack with soft drinks or Burmese tea.

Makes 5 servings.

The following two meatball dishes are usually fried and can be included in this section. However, grilling is an option, so I have shown this alternative. These dishes are very popular in restaurants and hotels. They are served as good snacks for beer. I include some chilies and curry powder to add extra spiciness to the dish.

In Burma, duck eggs are abundant and cheaper than chicken eggs. So they are used for cooking as they also provide better taste and flavor.

Chicken fillets can also be minced and prepared in the same way as minced pork (savory taste) or as minced beef (hot taste).

MINCED PORK BALLS

I prefer this dish fried but the choice is yours.

Ingredients
1 pound minced pork
1 small egg (duck or
    chicken), beaten and
    stirred
1 tablespoon cornstarch

3 cloves garlic, chopped
    or blended
½ tablespoon white wine
½ teaspoon white pepper
1 teaspoon salt
Oil for frying

Method
- Combine all the ingredients except oil in a bowl and mix well.
- Heat oil in a deep pan for frying.
- Scoop the minced pork mixture (about ½ tablespoon) and roll it into a ball.

To fry:: Put in the pan and fry in hot oil until golden brown. Remove and drain on paper towels.

To grill (alternative): Place each individual meatball on a broiler plate. Grill on medium heat and turn occasionally until golden brown.

- Continue to fry/grill until the mixture is finished.

To Serve: These entrées can be served with chili sauce and freshly squeezed lime juice.

Makes 4 servings.

MINCED BEEF BALLS

F or those who prefer beef, try this recipe.

Ingredients

1 pound minced beef
1 teaspoon salt
¼ teaspoon turmeric powder
1 tablespoon fish sauce
3 to 4 fresh chilies, chopped or blended
1 small onion, chopped or blended

3 cloves garlic, chopped or blended
1 tablespoon cornstarch
2 teaspoons curry powder
1 teaspoon sweet paprika
6 mint leaves, chopped
Oil for frying

Method

- Combine all ingredients except oil in a bowl and mix well.
- Heat oil in a frying pan.
- Scoop the minced beef mixture (about ½ tablespoon) and roll into a ball.

To fry: Put in the pan and fry over hot oil until golden brown. Remove and drain on paper towels.

To grill (alternative): Place each individual meatball on a broiler plate. Grill on medium heat and turn occasionally until golden brown.

- Continue to fry until the mixture is finished.

To Serve: These entrées can be served with chili sauce and freshly squeezed lime juice.

Makes 4 servings.

DESSERTS AND MORNING TREATS: A-CHO

DESSERTS AND MORNING TREATS: A-CHO

A-cho refers to anything that is sweet, especially desserts. Burmese people enjoy some sweet and delicious treats after their meals. In fact, they can eat desserts at any time of the day. The most popular dessert is probably Semolina Cake (page 181).

In this section, I have also included a popular morning treat, Steamed Glutinous Rice with Nuts (page 183). In Burma, this dish is regarded as a simple treat for poorer people. Of course, things are not always what they seem—bread and butter, for example, is seen as a delicacy for the middle class. Now that I am living in the West, my tastes are reversed and I prefer glutinous rice to bread and butter—any time!

SEMOLINA CAKE

This is a delicious cake made from dry-fried semolina seeds mixed with coconut and sugar. Dried grapes can be added for a sweeter taste.

Ingredients

1 cup semolina	1 cup milk
2 tablespoons butter	1 teaspoon salt
½ cup sugar	1 egg, beaten
1 can (12 ounces) coconut milk	1 tablespoon oil
	2 tablespoons poppy seed

Method

- In a nonstick pan, add semolina and dry-fry for about 5 minutes on low-medium heat until it turns reddish in color. Remove from the pan.
- Add butter to the pan. When butter is melted, add sugar, coconut milk, milk, and salt and stir well.
- Add in eggs and semolina and combine well into a smooth batter.
- Add oil in a nonstick wok. When hot, pour in the semolina batter and stir continuously for about 10 to 15 minutes over low heat until the liquid is almost dried out.
- Pour the mixture into a nonstick baking dish and flatten the surface with a spatula.
- Sprinkle with poppy seeds and broil on medium heat for 15 to 20 minutes until the mixture turns golden brown and crispy.

To Serve: Let it cool and cut into desired pieces and serve with tea or coffee.

Makes 8 servings.

BURMESE COCONUT PORRIDGE

This sweet porridge is usually eaten on winter nights. It is not eaten in large quantities; only a small rice bowl is served as dessert. Of course, second servings are most welcome.

The secret to this porridge is the addition of salt. Try to taste the porridge just before and after adding the salt and note the difference. The porridge is not complete until salt is added.

Ingredients
½ cup white rice
1 small can (4 ounces)
   coconut milk
⅓ cup white sugar
⅓ teaspoon salt

Method
- Soak the rice in water for 30 minutes, then drain.
- Boil rice with 5½ cups water in a pot. Do not cover, as rice water will spill. Boil on medium heat for about 25 minutes until rice is dissolved or grains disappear. Stir the porridge mixture occasionally.
- Add coconut milk and sugar and bring to boil. Reduce heat and simmer for an additional 15 minutes to bring out the coconut flavor.
- Add salt to porridge.

To Serve: Serve with more salt or sugar depending on personal taste.

Makes 4 servings.

STEAMED GLUTINOUS RICE WITH NUTS

This is one of the morning breakfast treats that is sold in most places. The glutinous rice is placed inside a large piece of cotton material, in a large bamboo basket to keep warm. The glutinous rice is scooped onto the banana leaf and served with roasted and pounded sesame and salt mixture and freshly grated coconut flesh.

Traditionally, the soaked rice and black-eyed peas are mixed together and placed inside a clean piece of cloth and steamed.

My friend Mai gave me a great glutinous rice steamer, the design of which is based on traditional Laotian cookware. I have seen these for sale in Thai grocery stores and would recommend them for this purpose. This rice steamer comes in two parts, sold separately. The first part is a metal pot, shaped like a large vase, which is filled with water for steaming. The second part is a bamboo basket, shaped like a cone, in which the rice and beans are placed. You should cover the contents with an ordinary saucepan lid.

Ingredients
3 cups glutinous rice
1 cup dried black-eyed peas
¼ cup sesame seed

2 teaspoons salt
1 fresh coconut, grated

Method
- Wash the rice and beans and soak in water overnight. Drain.
- Place the glutinous rice and beans in the bamboo cone. Mix well, cover and steam using the steamer on medium-high heat.
- After 20 minutes, remove the saucepan lid cover. Using both hands, one on each side, take out the bamboo cone basket. Flip the contents upside down.

Continued

- Return the bamboo cone, cover and continue to steam for another 15 minutes over medium-high heat.
- While the rice is steaming, pan-fry the sesame seeds and salt in a nonstick frying pan for about 5 minutes or until sesame seeds are golden brown.
- Remove the sesame seeds and salt mixture to a mortar and pound well with a pestle.

To Serve: Traditionally, the steamed glutinous rice is served with a dash of roasted and pounded sesame and salt mixture and freshly grated coconut. However, as a breakfast dish, usual accompaniments are assorted fritters, fried fish, meat, or even Fried Shrimp with Shrimp Paste (page 146).

Makes 6 to 8 servings.

SAGO AND SWEET POTATO WITH COCONUT MILK

This is a nice sweet dessert to be served during winter nights. I will usually prepare this dessert when I have a craving for something sweet. Sago pearls are similar to tapioca, and have to be soaked before use.

Ingredients

½ cup sago pearls
2 medium sweet potatoes,
   cut into ¼ inch cubes
½ cup white sugar
1 cup water
¼ teaspoon salt
1 small can (4 ounces)
   coconut milk

Method

- Wash sago and soak in water for 1 hour.
- Put sweet potato and 3 cups water in a pot and boil on high heat for about 15 minutes or until potatoes are soft.
- Add sago and boil for about 10 minutes until the sago pearls are transparent.
- Add sugar, milk, salt, and coconut milk and continue to boil for 10 minutes on low-medium heat, stirring occasionally.

To Serve: Serve late on a winter night, after dinner has been digested. Serve with more sugar if sweeter taste is preferred.

Makes 4 servings.

COCONUT AND BUTTER GLUTINOUS RICE CAKE

This is another sweet cake made out of glutinous rice with coconut and sugar. A must to try for those with a sweet tooth.

Ingredients

2 cups glutinous rice, washed and soaked overnight

1 tablespoon oil

2 teaspoons butter

1 can (12 ounces) coconut milk

1 cup white sugar

¼ teaspoon salt

Method

- Wash the rice and soak overnight. Drain.
- Preheat oven to 400°F (200°C).
- Add oil and butter in a nonstick saucepan. Add the glutinous rice and fry over medium heat for about 2 minutes.
- Add in coconut milk, sugar, and salt and stir well for about 3 minutes on medium heat.
- Reduce to low heat, cover, and simmer for about 12 minutes or until rice is cooked.
- Pour the glutinous rice in a greased tin and press it with a flat spatula to form a smooth surface.
- Bake the glutinous rice in oven for 15 to 20 minutes until the top layer is golden brown and crispy.

To Serve: Let it cool before cutting into desired shapes and enjoy with tea or coffee.

Makes 8 servings.

TRADITIONAL BURMESE TEA SALAD AND TEA: LEPHET-THOKE

TRADITIONAL BURMESE TEA SALAD AND TEA: LEPHET-THOKE

This traditional dish is quite unique. It is enjoyed by people of any age everywhere in Burma. For example, girls whether they live in country or city, love to eat this dish in a gathering with friends and gossip at the same time. Older people also have this dish with Burmese tea during conversations.

It can be eaten after lunch or dinner, much like the Western tradition of cake and tea/coffee. Burmese Tea Salad has some degree of caffeine and therefore it is quite a stimulant. Some people who eat this dish during the night claim that they can not sleep properly, it does not stop me.

The Burmese tea mixture used in this salad consists of hand-picked young and tender tea leaves, garlic, beans, peas, sesame seeds, and peanuts. The tea leaves are treated with salt and sesame oil to make them soft, fine, and very fragrant. Garlic is sliced and fried until crisp and golden brown. The broad beans and split peas are fried until crunchy. Peanuts and sesame seeds are roasted until fragrant.

The salad mixture is put in a bowl and a teaspoon is provided for each person to scoop and eat from the same salad bowl. Usually it is made very hot by adding lots of freshly diced chilies or biting fresh chilies in between each teaspoonful of tea salad. It is usually accompanied by Burmese tea.

Burmese tea leaves used for drinking are bigger than those in the salad and have been roasted until very fragrant and are usually quite strong. The strong and bitter taste of the tea goes extremely well with this salad.

Ingredients for this Burmese tea salad are usually bought ready-made. Try them when you are in Burma or alternatively, contact me through my website, www.myanmar.com.au.

BURMESE TEA SALAD

Ingredients

1 pack ready-made Burmese
  tea mixture
1 teaspoon fish sauce
2 teaspoons lime juice
2 to 3 fresh chilies, diced
  or cut into small pieces

¼ cup dried shrimp, wash
  and drained
2 tablespoons oil

Method
- Put all ingredients in a bowl and mix well.

To Serve: Best to serve with fresh hot chilies and Burmese tea.

Makes 4 to 6 servings.

SPECIAL OCCASIONS

COCONUT CHICKEN NOODLE SOUP

This is a very popular soup to serve on special occasions such as traditional Burmese weddings or birthdays. The giant soup pot can be as big as 26 gallons or more, filled with lots of chicken pieces and floating small onions.

Traditionally in Burma, coconut meat is grated from the fresh coconut first. Then it is boiled with hot water and poured into a cloth to squeeze the fresh milk out. This is troublesome but adds a fresh taste, aroma, and extra creaminess to the soup. In my opinion, canned coconut milk is no match for the freshly grated and squeezed coconut juice.

However, in Western countries coconut milk is easily obtainable from the markets. As we are very busy with our life schedules, we constantly search for ways to get things done in an easier way. I now just buy cans of coconut milk for cooking.

In Burma different types of noodles are used with this dish. At home, I use noodles that most closely resemble and taste like those from Burma. These are the Hokkien egg noodles (thick style) and the Italian spaghetti.

Note: While serving, just enough soup is added to cover the noodles. Thus, soup is seldom left behind once the noodles have been eaten. The Burmese serve the noodles with a spoon only but of course our Western friends use forks or chopsticks.

Traditionally, this soup is left to simmer for many hours over a low heat. This process brings out the full taste and smell of the delicious ingredients: chicken, chickpeas and coconut. At home, we generally prepare smaller quantities but we still like to bring out the full flavor by re-heating the soup. Towards the end of the pot, the last servings taste so good that it encourages us to cook the dish again next time.

Recipe and ingredients on next page

Ingredients

1 cup chickpea flour, mixed into smooth batter with 2 cups water
4 tablespoons oil
¼ teaspoon turmeric powder
2 teaspoons sweet paprika
1 chicken (2½ to 3 pounds), cut into small pieces (½ inch)
¼ cup fish sauce
8 large onions, halved
1 small piece (¼ inch) fresh ginger, cut into small pieces
2 cans (around 30 ounces) coconut milk
2 fried onions (page 109)

2 teaspoons salt
6 boiled eggs, hard boiled and sliced
2 packages Chinese egg noodles (16 ounces each)

Garnish

1 bunch Chinese parsley, finely chopped
2 onions, washed, drained, and finely sliced
Juice of 1 lemon
Fish sauce
Fresh chili powder

Method

- Add 16 cups water to a soup pot and bring to boil. Pour in the split pea batter and stir occasionally to avoid burning. Reduce heat and continue to boil.
- Heat oil in frying pan, add turmeric powder and paprika and sauté on low heat for 2 minutes.
- Increase to high heat and add chicken pieces and fry well for 3 minutes.
- Add fish sauce and mix for 1 minute.
- Pour the chicken mixture into the soup pot. Add onions and ginger and continue to boil in low-medium heat for 1 hour, stirring occasionally.

- Add in coconut milk, fried onions, and salt and continue to simmer for 45 minutes. Add boiled egg slices and simmer for 15 minutes.
- In a separate pot, boil water. Cook noodles 2 to 3 minutes. Put in a strainer and rinse with cold water.

To Serve: For each serving, put some noodles in a bowl and add enough soup to cover the noodles. Serve soup noodle with chopped parsley, thinly sliced onion rings, lemon juice, fish sauce, and chili powder.

Makes 8 servings.

The traditional noodle that is served in Burma is called *mouk-hin-kar*. It has a slightly sour taste and hence the dish is named as such. This is also a favorite Burmese breakfast dish.

In the market and at the street stalls, this noodle is available from morning to the evening, usually contained in a large pot of 26 gallons or more. The aroma of the soup can be smelled from afar. On closer look, the soup is filled with thinly sliced banana trunks and floating whole baby onions.

Catfish is used for cooking *mouk-hin-kar* in Burma. Although, it looks a bit scary, it makes the best soup stock. Alternatively, flathead fish can be used instead of catfish.

A generous amount of ginger is used and naturally fish sauce is the main ingredient in this fish soup. The fish bones are reboiled a couple of times to make fish stock. In Burma, people usually pound all the bones using a mortar and pestle and the bones are then boiled to bring out the sweetness of the fish. Onions and garlic are generously used in this dish to add flavor and to overcome the fishy smell.

Another interesting main ingredient is the banana heart, the young and tender part of the freshly chopped banana tree trunk. Several outer layers of the trunks or stems are peeled away leaving only the soft, tender and young stem. Of course, it is not easy to get this banana heart. We used to ask our neighbor for some banana trees. We chopped the tree just to get the heart for cooking. These days, we have adapted well and can live without the banana heart.

To make the soup thick, the coarse rice flour available in Indian shops is better than the smooth rice flour found in Chinese shops. It is best to serve this soup using Italian yellow egg noodles, Japanese (*somen*) noodles, and/or Chinese thick rice (*hor-fun*) noodle.

Since this dish requires a lot of effort to prepare, you need at least one person to help you. Usually when the fish is being boiled, I roast the rice flour, boil the noodle and eggs, etc. My mum helps me to prepare the onion, garlic, parsley, cut the rice noodles, etc. It is quite time consuming and it is much more fun if you chat with someone and listen to music while cooking.

To those who want to try some, but do not wish to cook a lot, please use only half or third of the ingredients listed below. This dish is best accompanied by Fried Split Peas (page 170) to add crunchiness to the soup. It is necessary to soak the peas in cold water with some baking powder the night before cooking.

Ingredients

4 pounds flathead fish or silver bream
3 big pieces fresh ginger (6 ounces)
5 stalks lemongrass
1½ cups fish sauce
2 teaspoons turmeric powder
2 cups rice flour
2 pounds small onions, skins peeled
1 whole head garlic
1 slice (¼ inch) fish paste
⅓ cup oil
2½ tablespoons sweet paprika
2 teaspoons salt
2 teaspoons crushed black pepper
1 package (16 ounces) Chinese thick egg noodles (Hokkien) or Japanese *somen*, or both

To Serve

6 eggs, hard boiled and sliced
1 bunch Chinese parsley, washed, dried and finely chopped
Fried split peas (page 170)
Juice of 2 lemons
Fish sauce
Fresh chili powder

Method

Initial preparation
- Scale the fish, wash and drain.
- Remove the ginger skin and pound lightly. Cut into several pieces.
- Lightly pound the lemongrass and cut each into 3 pieces.

Continued

To make fish stock
- In a big soup pot, add 3 quarts water, pounded ginger, 1 cup fish sauce, 4 pounded lemongrass, and 1 teaspoon of turmeric powder and boil for about 15 minutes over high heat.
- Add fish and boil for 15 minutes over high heat, uncovered to avoid soup from spilling.
- Reduce to medium heat and continue to boil for 30 minutes. Meanwhile prepare other ingredients.

To make rice flour batter (while fish is boiling)
- Roast the rice flour in a saucepan over low heat for about 10 minutes stirring continuously to avoid burning the flour. Remove the pan and allow the rice flour to cool (about 15 minutes).
- Put the flour in a big bowl and add 3 cups cold water gradually. Mix into a smooth batter and put aside.

To thicken fish stock (when fish boiling time is up)
- Remove fish and lemongrass from the soup pot.
- Add the rice flour batter into the fish stock and stir well until the soup is a medium consistency (not too thick or too watery) and bring to a boil. Reduce heat and continue to boil uncovered.
- Scoop the batter bubbles from the surface of the soup occasionally.

Continue to make more fish stock
- When the fish has cooled, separate the fish fillets from the bones.
- Put bones in a small pot, add 4 cups of boiled hot water and let it boil over medium heat to make more fish stock. Press the fish bones with a spatula gently and boil for 15 minutes.
- Transfer stock to the fish soup pot using a strainer. Take care not to drop the bones into the fish soup pot.
- Continue this process for one more time to prepare fish stock and add to the fish soup pot.

To fry the fish mixture (when fish stock has been prepared)

- Put 2 onions aside. Add the rest of onions to the fish soup pot.
- Slice the 2 reserved onions finely.
- Peel, crush, and chop the garlic finely.
- Slice 1 lemongrass root finely. Use the white part only.
- Dissolve shrimp paste in 3 tablespoons warm water.
- In a frying pan, add the oil, sliced onions, chopped garlic, and sliced lemongrass and fry over low-medium heat for about 10 minutes or until fragrant.
- Add paprika, 1 teaspoon turmeric powder, fish fillets, and shrimp paste solution and stir well for 5 minutes.
- Add ½ cup fish sauce and mix well for about 2 minutes.

Continue to cook the fish soup

- Remove the fried fish mixture and transfer to the fish soup pot, stir well, and bring to a boil.
- Reduce heat and add salt, pepper to the fish soup pot and continue to boil over low heat for 1 to 2 hours, stirring occasionally to avoid sticking to the pot. The longer the soup is simmered, the better it tastes.

Prepare Noodles

- Cook noodles in boiling water. Rinse in cold water and drain.

To Serve: For each serving, put some noodles in a medium bowl and add enough fish soup to cover the noodles. Serve fish soup with 2 egg slices, chopped parsley, fried split peas, lemon juice, fish sauce (if required) and fresh chili powder. Note: Soup is always served piping hot.

Makes 10 to 12 servings.

HAND-MIXED NOODLE SALAD

This is another weekend dish, and one to be prepared with some helpers. It involves a lot of washing, chopping and cutting the various vegetables as well as preparing the accompanying soup.

This is a delightful dish to enjoy during summertime as it involves a lot of green vegetables. All the vegetables and ingredients are pre-

pared and placed on different plates. To serve it, each person takes the desired amount of each ingredient and adjusts the taste accordingly. I have put down a basic guide on how much to put for each ingredient accord-

ing to my taste. As there are so many ingredients to this dish, before you realize it, your plate is already full. So just take a bit of each ingredient and make sure that they all blend well with the fish sauce and tamarind sauce.

This is a very colorful dish, with yellow noodles, tofu, potatoes, bean sprouts and onion oil; purple onions, green vegetables; brown tamarind sauce; and red chili powder.

Traditionally, all the ingredients are put on a big plate and we use our fingers to mix and eat. This is truly a finger-licking dish and hence the name Hand-Mixed Noodle Salad. This dish shows that each person has individual taste. Usually, we try about a tablespoon of each other's noodle and compare and compete to see who has prepared a better taste. Of course, for those who are strangers to this custom, use a spoon, fork or chopsticks to mix the ingredients and serve. The Pepper and Garlic Fish Soup with Vermicelli (page 155) or Simple Shrimp and Vermicelli Soup (page 157) best accompanies this dish.

Ingredients

2 packages (15 ounces each) Chinese thick egg noodles (Hokkien)
1 package (16 ounces) bean sprouts
6 medium potatoes
2 cups oil
1 package (16 ounces) firm tofu
1 package (7 ounces) frozen fish cakes
½ teaspoon turmeric powder
3 big brown onions, finely sliced
1 cup chickpea flour
2 big purple onions
1 big knuckle of tamarind
2 cucumbers
1 package (6 ounces) dried shrimp, blended or pounded
1 cup fish sauce
1 bunch parsley, washed, drained and finely chopped.
¼ cup cabbage, finely sliced
Chili powder

Method

- Boil noodles in a small pan, rinse in cold water and drain.
- Boil bean sprouts in hot water quickly for 30 seconds and remove and drain.
- Boil potatoes in a saucepan until soft, slice.
- Heat 2 tablespoons oil in a frying pan and add tofu and fry. Remove tofu and slice finely.
- Add fish cakes to the frying pan and fry for 3 minutes on each side. Remove fish cakes and slice finely.
- Heat remaining oil in the same pan. Add turmeric powder and sliced brown onions and fry until golden brown. Remove onions and drain. Pour oil in a bowl.
- In a clean dry pan, dry-fry the chickpea flour until golden brown. Put in a bowl and let cool.
- Slice purple onions thin and sprinkle with sugar; wash, drain and set aside.
- Wash tamarind and soak in 3 cups hot water for 15 minutes. Squeeze tamarind in water to extract juice. Set aside.
- Cut cucumbers into thin strips.

Continued

To Serve: Let guests create their own mixtures. Here is my suggestion for each serving: In a big plate, add a handful of noodles, few potato slices, 1 tablespoon cucumber, a handful of bean sprouts, tofu, fish cake slices, purple onion, ½ tablespoon pounded shrimp, 1 tablespoon fried onion, 2 teaspoons of fish sauce, 1 teaspoon fried onion oil, 2 tablespoons of tamarind sauce, 1 teaspoon chickpea flour, ½ tablespoon parsley, and some cabbage.

Mix all the ingredients and taste. Add chili powder for hotter taste. Add more fish sauce (salty) or tamarind sauce (sour), chili (hot) or other ingredients according to individual taste.

Serve with Pepper and Garlic Fish Soup with Vermicelli (page 155) or Simple Shrimp and Vermicelli Soup (page 157).

Makes 10 to 12 servings.

SPECIAL TAMARIND, CHILI AND GARLIC SAUCE

This is a strong sauce due to large amounts of garlic and chilies. It is only for those who want to experience authentic Burmese flavors. However, the result is definitely worth the effort as it brings more exotic flavors to the Hand-Mixed Noodle Salad (page 202).

Ingredients
2 whole heads garlic
8 to 10 fresh chilies
7 ounces tamarind
½ teaspoon sweet paprika
1 teaspoon salt
4 teaspoons sugar
1 tablespoon Chinese light
   soy sauce
1 tablespoon black or white
   vinegar
2 stalks Chinese parsley,
   finely chopped

Method
- Remove skin from garlic. Dry-fry garlic and chilies over low heat for about 4 minutes or until fragrant.
- Soak tamarind in a bowl with 3 cups hot water for about 10 minutes.
- Mix tamarind and water using the hand or mesh the tamarind using a wooden spatula to make tamarind juice. Leave the tamarind pulps in the bowl.
- Pound roasted garlic and chilies well and add mixture to the tamarind juice.
- Add paprika, salt, sugar, soy sauce, vinegar, and parsley and stir well.

To Serve: This sauce is to serve with the Hand-Mixed Noodle Salad (page 202) or any fritters (pages 165-176).

Makes 3 cups.

GARLIC OIL

This is garlic cooked in hot oil with some turmeric powder. I have to include this garlic oil recipe here because this is a very important ingredient to be used in the next dish, the Mandalay Chicken Noodles. This particular dish needs the golden look from the fried garlic oil in turmeric powder to brighten up the dish along with the curry chicken gravy sauces.

Please note that this recipe produces "garlic in oil". Some dishes may require the garlic or the oil as separate ingredients. Other dishes may require both the garlic and the oil to be used.

Ingredients
1 whole head garlic
½ cup oil
2 teaspoons turmeric powder

Method
- Remove garlic skin and chop or dice with the knife or chopper very fine. If using the blender do not overblend.
- Add oil to a small pot and heat it on medium heat.
- When oil is hot, reduce to low heat and add turmeric powder, and garlic and fry until golden brown. Lightly stir the garlic continuously to avoid burning but allow a little browning. Switch off heat when it starts to get brown, as the hot oil will continue to cook it further.

To Serve: Serve with the Mandalay Chicken Noodle (page 207).

Makes ½ cup.

MANDALAY CHICKEN NOODLE

This noodle dish originated in Mandalay, and is also known as Mandalay noodle or Mandalay *Mouti*. Mandalay is the second largest city in Burma located in upper Myanmar. This is a very popular dish enjoyed by people in Yangoon as well.

The noodles are mixed with curry chicken and vegetables and are accompanied by Chicken and Tomato Soup (page 159), topped with pepper.

Note that the curry chicken sauce is a bit watery because it will be served with the noodles. The roasted chickpea flour soaks up the liquid and enhances the noodle taste. The noodle mixture should have golden color due to the chili and turmeric powder and from garlic oil.

Ingredients

2 chicken breasts
5½ tablespoons oil
2 medium onions, finely chopped
6 cloves garlic, finely chopped
1 small piece (¼ inch) fresh ginger, cut into small slices or cubes
1 teaspoon salt

Marinade

3½ tablespoons fish sauce
1½ tablespoons sweet paprika
1 tablespoon turmeric powder
1 tablespoon curry powder

Other Ingredients

2 packages standard spaghetti
1 pound French beans
1 package (15 ounces) bean sprout
1 bunch Chinese parsley, finely chopped
Fish sauce
1 cup roasted chickpea powder (page 110)
Juice of 1 lemon
½ cup garlic oil (page 206)
Fresh chili powder (optional)

Continued

Method

- Cut chicken breasts into small cubes and soak in the marinade with the ingredients for about 15 minutes.
- Heat oil in a saucepan. Add onions, 2 teaspoons chopped garlic, and ginger, and fry over medium heat for about 5 minutes until onions are transparent.
- Add marinated chicken mixture and fry for 6 minutes.
- Add salt and 1½ cups water, cover and bring to a boil. Reduce to low heat and simmer for about 15 minutes.
- Cook spaghetti according to package instructions, drain.
- Cook beans in boiling water until tender. Cut into small slices.
- Cook bean sprouts in boiling water for ½ minute and drain.

To Serve: For each serving, use a large plate or bowl. Add a handful of noodles and 3 to 4 tablespoons curry chicken sauce, 1 tablespoon chopped beans, 1 tablespoon bean sprouts, 1 teaspoon parsley, ¼ teaspoon fish sauce, 1 teaspoon roasted chickpea flour, ¼ teaspoon lemon juice, ½ teaspoon fried garlic, and ½ teaspoon garlic oil.

Mix all the ingredients and taste. Add more fish sauce or lemon juice or chilie powder according to taste. Serve with Chicken Tomato Soup (page 159).

Makes 12 to 15 servings.

SWEET AND SOUR TAMARIND JUICE

This is a refreshing drink that also aids the digestion of food. The traditional sugar used for this drink is made from palm juice and hence it is called palm sugar. Along the countryside in Bagan, men climb up the palm tree to get palm fruits and the women cook the palm sugar alongside the trees in a thatched hut with one big wok. Talking to them, we found out that the fresh palm juice is poured into a big wok and stirred continuously for over half an hour to form palm sugar syrup. About half a tablespoon of syrup is then scooped and rolled into a ball, which is about the size of a chocolate. The palm sugar balls are allowed to cool and form hard sugar nuggets.

This palm sugar nugget is the traditional Burmese confection, served after meals. In the country areas, the host always serves this palm sugar nugget to welcome visitors.

Ingredients
¼ package (3 to 4 ounces) tamarind
1 cup sugar, palm or brown preferred
1 teaspoon salt
4 cups cool spring water
1 carton or tray ice cubes

Method
- Wash tamarind and soak in 1 cup hot water for ½ hour. Press or squeeze the tamarind pulp and strain juice into a jug.
- Boil or dissolve sugar in ½ cup hot water. Add the sugar solution, salt, and 2½ cups water to the tamarind juice in the jug. Stir well.
- Dilute with ⅓ cup water or add more sugar as desired. For extra sourness, add more tamarind juice.

To Serve: Add ice cubes just before serving.

Makes 4 to 6 servings.

AVOCADO DRINK

The avocados in Burma are big, very round, and brown/black. This is an ideal drink during hot summer days and I especially like the crushed ice mixed with the smooth taste of avocado. This is my father's favorite drink. During the avocado season, he will make this every night after dinner until he gets sick of it.

Ingredients
1 ripe avocado
4 tablespoons sugar
3 cups milk
1 carton or tray ice cubes

Method
- Scoop out the avocado flesh and put into a blender.
- Combine all the ingredients and blend until the ice cubes are crushed.

To Serve: Pour in glasses and serve with more ice cubes if desired.

Makes 4 servings.

INDEX

A

Avocado
  Avocado Drink, 212

B

Bamboo Shoots
  Pork with Bamboo Shoots, 100
  Roselle Leaves with Shrimp, 99
Banana, Ladyfinger
  Assorted Vegetable Fritters, 169
Banana Leaf, Dried
  Pepper and Garlic Fish Soup
    with Vermicelli, 155
  Simple Shrimp and Vermicelli
    Soup, 157
Bay Leaf
  Split Pea and Prawn Soup, 158
Bean Sprout
  Firm Tofu with Bean Sprouts,
    136
  Hand-Mixed Noodle Salad, 203
  Mandalay Chicken Noodle, 207
  Shrimp with Bean Sprout
    Fritters, 171
Beef
  Beef Curry with Coconut Milk,
    80
  Beef Curry with Fish Paste, 68
  Beef Curry with Yogurt, 81
  Fried Beef Slices with Curry
    Powder, 130
  Fried Minced Pork Balls, 175

Bitter Melon
  Fried Bitter Melon with Prawns,
    125
Black-Eyed Pea
  Steamed Glutinous Rice with
    Nuts, 183
Butter
  Coconut and Butter Glutinous
    Rice Cake, 186
  Red lentil and Butter Rice, 52
  Semolina Cake, 181

C

Cabbage
  Hand-Mixed Noodle Salad, 203
  Pork Fillets with Mixed
    Vegetables, 128
  Sweet and Sour Tomato and
    Cabbage Pickles, 145
Capsicum
  Pork Fillets with Mixed
    Vegetables, 128
Carrot
  Mixed Vegetable Curry, 79
  Pork Fillets with Mixed
    Vegetables, 128
Chicken
  Chicken Curry with Coconut
    Milk, 67
  Chicken Curry with Gourd in
    Thin Sauce, 65
  Chicken Curry with Gravy
    Sauce, 63

Curry (continued)
    Mixed Vegetable Curry, 79
    Pork Curry with Tamarind, 71
    Prawn Curry, 69
Curry Powder
    Fried Beef Slices with Curry
        Powder, 130
    Fried Minced Pork Balls, 175

D

Dessert
    Burmese Coconut Porridge, 182
    Coconut and Butter Glutinous
        Rice Cake, 186
    Sago and Sweet Potato with
        Coconut Milk, 185
    Semolina Cake, 181
    Steamed Glutinous Rice with
        Nuts, 183
Dips
    Chili Tomato Sauce, 143
    Dried Shrimp and Fish Sauce
        Dip, 148
    Fried Shrimps with Shrimp
        Paste, 146
    Instant Fish Sauce Dip, 150
    Pounded Grilled Shrimp Paste
        and Garlic, 149
    Sweet and Sour Cucumber, 144
    Sweet and Sour Tomato and
        Cabbage Pickles, 145
Drinks
    Avocado Drink, 212
    Sweet and Sour Tamarind Juice,
        211
Duck
    Duck Curry, 82

E

Egg
    Coconut Chicken Noodle Soup,
        195
    Egg Curry with Dried Shrimps,
        73
    Hot and Sour Soup, 160
    Minced Pork Balls, 175
    Rice Noodles with Fish Soup,
        199
    Semolina Cake, 181
Eggplant
    Fish Cake and Mixed
        Vegetables with Tamarind, 102
    Fried eggplants with Shrimp, 127
    Grilled Eggplant Salad, 120
    Mixed Vegetable Curry, 79

F

Fermented Mustard
    Pork Spareribs and Fermented
        Mustard Soup, 164
Fish
    Double Fried Fish Curry, 61
    Fish Cake Salad, 112
    Fish with White Radish, 101
    Pepper and Garlic Fish Soup
        with Vermicelli 155
    Rice Noodles with Fish Soup,
        199
    Special Steamed Hilsha Fish, 91
    Steamed Fish with Onions and
        Chilies, 93
Fish Ball
    Hot and Sour Soup, 160

Glutinous Rice (continued)
  Steamed Glutinous Rice with
    Nuts, 183
Glutinous Rice Flour
  Assorted Vegetable Fritters, 169
  Fried Split Peas, 170
  Shrimp with Bean Sprouts
    Fritters, 171
Gourd
  Assorted Vegetable Fritters, 169
  Chicken with Gourd in Thin
    Sauce, 65
  Fried Gourd with Shrimp, 135
  Mixed Vegetable Curry, 79

H

Hilsha Fish
  Special Steamed Hilsha Fish, 91

L

Lamb
  Lamb Curry with Split Peas, 84
Lemon
  Lemon and Onions Salad, 113
Lemongrass
  Chicken Curry with potatoes
    and Lemongrass,86
  Hot and Sour Soup, 160
  Rice Noodles with Fish Soup, 199
  Special Seamed Hilsha Fish, 91
Long Beans
  Mixed Vegetable Curry, 79

M

Mango
  Mango Salad, 114
Milk
  Semolina Cake, 181
  Avocado Drink, 212
Mint Leaves
  Fried Beef Slices with Curry
    Powder, 130
  Fried Yellow Split Pea Cake, 173
  Minced Beef Balls, 176

N

Noodles
  Coconut Chicken Noodle Soup,
    195
  Hand-Mixed Noodle Salad, 203
  Mandalay Chicken Noodle, 207
  Rice Noodles with Fish Soup, 199

O

Ocean Perch Fish
  Fish with White Radish, 101
Okra
  Fish Cake and Mixed
    Vegetables with Tamarind, 102
Onion
  Assorted Vegetable Fritters, 169
  Fried Onions, 109
  Lemon and Onions Salad, 113
  Steamed Fish with Onion and
    Chilies, 93
Onions, Fried
  Fried Onions, 109
  Coconut Chicken Noodle Soup,
    195

Also available from Hippocrene ...

The Best of Regional Thai Cuisine
Chat Mingkwan
Thai people have taken the best of culinary influences from nearby countries such as China, India, Cambodia, Indonesia, Laos, Malaysia, Burma and Vietnam, and adapted them to produce distinctly Thai creations like Galangal Chicken, Green Curry Chicken, and Three Flavor Prawns.

In addition to more than 150 recipes, all adapted for the North American kitchen, Chef Mingkwan provides helpful sections on Thai spices and ingredients as well as cooking techniques.
216 PAGES • 6 X 9 • 0-7818-0880-4 • $24.95HC • (26)

Thai-English/English-Thai Dictionary & Phrasebook
James Higbie
Thai belongs to the Tai language family, a group of related languages spoken in Thailand and Laos and by minority ethnic groups in Burma, northern Vietnam and southern China. This book provides a basic grammar, and the vocabulary and phrases a traveler might want to know. All Thai words are spelled in the English alphabet only, thus making it an easy reference for people unfamiliar with Thai script.
2,500 ENTRIES • 197 PAGES • 3¾ X 7½ • 0-7818-0774-3 • $12.95PB • (330)

Lao-English/English-Lao Dictionary & Phrasebook
James Higbie
Designed for travelers and people living in Laos and northeastern Thailand, this dictionary and phrasebook features the phrases and vocabulary of modern, spoken Lao. The two-way dictionary contains over 2,500 entries; the 49-section phrasebook provides practical cultural information and the means for communication in daily life and travel-related situations. Each Lao word is romanized, and pronunciation is indicated as well. The Lao language, also called Isan, has over 15 million speakers.
2,500 ENTRIES • 206 PAGES • 3¾ X 7½ • 0-7818-0858-8 • $12.95PB • (179)

Lao Basic Course
Warren G. Yates and Souksomboun Sayasithsena
This course is designed to give students a general proficiency in conversational Lao. Short lessons introduce students to basic grammar and vocabulary while exercises reinforce newly-introduced concepts. Each section contains helpful notes on special difficulties in the language.
423 PAGES • 5½ X 8½ • 0-7818-0410-8 • $19.95PB • (470)

All prices subject to change without prior notice. To purchase Hippocrene Books contact your local bookstore, call (718) 454-2366, visit www.hippocrenebooks.com, or write to: HIPPOCRENE BOOKS, 171 Madison Avenue, New York, NY 10016. Please enclose check or money order, adding $5.00 shipping (UPS) for the first book and $.50 for each additional book.